The Kingdom of God

"Your kingdom is an everlasting kingdom, and Your dominion endures throughout all generations." Psalm 145:13

"They tell of the glory of your kingdom and speak of Your might..." Psalm 145:11

Joseph D. Thornton, Th.D.

The Kingdom of God
Authority to Rule Over All Nations

Joseph D. Thornton, Th.D.

Copyright © 2018 by Joseph Thornton, Th.D.

ISBN 978-1-61529-196-0

All rights reserved world-wide.

No part of this book may be reproduced in any manner without the written permission of the author except in brief quotations embodied in critical articles of review.

Vision Publishing
P.O. Box 1680
Ramona, CA 92065
1 (760) 789-4700
www.booksbyvision.org

This book is dedicated in memory of my darling wife Katheryne to whom I was married for 66 years. Katheryne faithfully stood by my side, as a living example of all that a "virtuous woman" should be. She was a joy to our whole family, praying for and nurturing all of us. She never complained during the lean years and always encouraged us with her loving kindness. The memory of Katheryne stays fresh in our minds every day.

My beloved is mine, and I am his... (Song of Solomon 2:16)

You have gone now to receive your crown of righteousness; you fought a good fight and finished the race in style.

To dedicate this book in memory of you gives me great joy. Your life will always be a living testimony for generations to come.

- Joseph -

Table of Contents

Acknowledgements 5
Recommendations 9
Foreword 11
Introduction 13
Chapter 1 The Church and The Kingdom 15
Chapter 2 The Kingdoms of this World as Foreseen by the Prophet Daniel 21
Chapter 3 The Kingdom of God Defined 27
Chapter 4 Lordship in the Kingdom 41
Chapter 5 The Timing and Birth of a Nation 47
Chapter 6 Two Kingdoms Clash 53
Chapter 7 Four Manifestations of the Kingdom of God 57
Chapter 8 Stages of Growth: Progression in the Kingdom 75
Conclusion 87
About the Author 89

Acknowledgements

During the "latter reign" outpouring that occurred in the 1940s, and for several years beyond, Pentecostal preachers began to question as to whether or not the "eschatological end time" teaching was scripturally founded.

Thanks to the men of God who in these early years of my ministry were the first to introduce me to the message of "the present tense aspect of the Kingdom of God," and taught me to refrain from the "end time mentality" message that the evangelical church world so strongly embraced.

Dr. Leonard Coote and his son David Coote taught us that just because someone claimed a doctrine to be truth, does not necessarily make it truth. Both Leonard and David have gone on to their reward and no doubt are singing the song of Moses and the Lamb around the throne of God.

Leonard Loftin, whose prayer life and ministry had a profound impact on my life and ministry. I was privileged and blessed to be included in his ministry, and to see hundreds of souls baptized with the Holy Spirit.

Evert Roberts influenced me to have a Kingdom worldview instead of an end-time mentality view.

Dr. Ken Chant, of Australia, is one of the great theologians of our day. Being allowed to spend time in fellowship with him was invaluable. His published teaching library material would enhance any man's library. (www.booksbyvision.org)

Hal Oxley, of Australia, who so graciously gave of his time to help me find direction in a time when I needed to know God's plan for our future ministry.

Dr. Raymond Biard, whose hunger for truth far outweighed many of the younger generation ministers, who saw the first racially integrated church in Jackson, Mississippi, during the time of the signing of the Civil Rights Bill. I was privileged to spend time with him, rejoicing together on the subject of the Kingdom of God. He was one of the first men of God who taught that "the Church" is an extension of the Abrahamic covenant and was the second manifestation of the Kingdom of God.

Dr. Roy Roberts, a son in the Gospel, who was brought to Christ, and established in ministry under the preaching of the "present tense aspect of the Kingdom of God." He gave me a specific and profound word of prophecy that kept me from making the wrong turn in my ministry.

Dr. Stan DeKoven, Vision International University, whose ministry has blessed us for so many years and helped me through the time of grief over the death of my darling wife Katheryne. He also embraced the "present tense" message of the Kingdom of God and is involved in world evangelism, traveling into dozens of nations, establishing apostolic ministry and planting bible colleges in multiple languages.

In addition, God used the following ministers to encourage me to write and did so without them even being aware of it.

Donnie Metcalf – Pastor, Desert Reign Assembly, Downy, CA

Murray Tannehill – a true son in the gospel, Louisiana, deceased.

Joshua Tannehill – son of Murray Tannehill, deceased.

Bernie and Linda Morris – Pastors, Lighthouse Christian Fellowship, Madera, CA

Joey Myers – a son in the gospel, Shady Bower Pentecostal Church, Walker, LA

Matt Studer – a son in the gospel who delighted himself in the message of the Kingdom of God.

Tim Marsh – a son in the gospel, evangelist, Australia.

Cliff Beard – apostle, Australia, deceased.

Gary Hensley – a son in the gospel, Pastor, Calvary Worship Center, Fresno, CA

Greg Steen – Elder, Liberty Christian Fellowship, Fresno, CA

Daniel Zabalza – a son in the gospel, Assistant Pastor, ordained as Pastor, Liberty Christian Fellowship, Fresno, CA deceased.

Sincere thanks to:

Jo Pruit, Kelly Hulsey, and Janice S. Williams who so faithfully gave of their time and support in typing and arranging this manuscript.

8

Recommendations

Simply invaluable! After the Bible, this book is the foundation for my growth as a man of God. I first met Pastor Joseph during a conference in 1999, and although I had no desire to attend his church, I knew that he possessed something I did not. And over the next ten months, the Holy Spirit kept reminding me until I surrendered and obeyed, and ultimately sat and served under him.

Since then, through his teaching and preaching on the kingdom of God, Pastor Joseph opened the spiritual eyes of this average Christian. He revealed to me such concepts as the present-tense aspect of the Kingdom of God, the difference between a church mentality and a kingdom mentality, what we lost in the garden (dominion), and the fact that we are meant to be rulers here on earth, not simply sojourners. This volume represents more than sixty years of one man's revelations, with an emphasis on the coexistence of two kingdoms, the Abrahamic covenant, the invaluable work of the Cross, and who we are in Christ. You will undoubtedly, like me, find yourself referring back to its pages time and time again.

This material should be required study in every Bible College and seminary, and is certainly a must-read for any believer pursuing the true knowledge of God and His kingdom!

Greg Steen, Elder
Liberty Christian Fellowship, Fresno, CA

Having been a young evangelist, long term Pastor, and an Apostolic Leader, Rev. Joseph Thornton is in a position to write this book as he has thought through the implications and lived out its precepts. He is a living legacy in the Kingdom of God. He has served His Master well.

In these pages, we have the New Testament concepts of the Kingdom of God, the Rule and Sphere written out in plain language. Those who read these pages will be stimulated, inspired, and challenged to consider the ramifications of our Lord's statement, "Repent, for the Kingdom of Heaven is at hand," Matthew 4:17, and the Apostolic mission of "preaching the kingdom of God," Acts 28:31.

Rev. Powell H. Lemons,
Fresno, CA

This is one of the most definitive works written on the Kingdom of God that you will ever find. It was under Dr. Thornton's teaching that I first began to understand the importance of the Kingdom of God in the teaching of Jesus and His disciples.

When you realize how many times Jesus spoke about the Kingdom, you will come to understand its place in the plan of God. The information that he shares in this book has formed the basis of many hours of teaching by me, and others in our church.

Gary Hensley, Senior Pastor
Calvary Worship Center, Fresno, CA

Foreword

With the best of books, the man and the message cannot be easily delineated. This is especially true in regard to my friend, apostle and mentor. Dr. Joseph Thornton.

Dr. Joe and his incredible bride Katheryne have had a wonderful, inspiring and impactful ministry in general, and have been a tremendous blessing to me and my family. In the late 1980's, Dr. Joe and Dr. Katheryne reestablished a local church in Fresno, CA, Liberty Christian Fellowship. As pastors with church planting and international experience, as traveling musical evangelists, they knew the importance of foundation building in the local church. Though they initially did not want to give up the glamour of the ministry on the road, they embraced this assignment of the Lord with a whole heart. They knew that worship would be a key the growth and strength of the church, along with strong preaching and teaching. Finally, he knew only too well the important mandate of discipling the people into their purpose, while constantly envisioning the next generation and further church planting. From the beginning, they were Kingdom focused and apostolically gifted. By the grace of God, I was to become a small part of the work in Fresno, teaching once a month or so in their local church-based bible college, with students that would eventually become leaders in church and community, one of which, our beloved Pastor Daniel Zabalza, who is now with the Lord…who became successor to Dr. Joe.

Many times when I would come and teach, I had the privilege of bringing my first wife Karen, who is now with the Lord. She always loved Liberty, but especially Pastor Joe, and he was like a father to her. The worship at Liberty was always outstanding, and tears of joy often came to my brides' heart during the worship time. Without question, Dr. Joe has a father's heart, one key to the ministry of a true apostle.

Over the years, I have had the opportunity of observing Dr. Joe as he modeled Kingdom wisdom and Kingdom authority. His road as a pastor and mentor too many has not been easy, but I can certainly say that it has been one filled with grace, much longsuffering, and a deep love for Christ, his word and the Kingdom. He has given himself to the message of the Kingdom, and in many ways, was prophetic in his preaching and teaching, as he was often ahead of his time. Thus, I can, without reservation, recommend this short but powerful work to the reader. It is not fancy, as neither is Joe, but it is filled with wisdom and the godly perspective we need today to see the church become what it has been already declared to be, a bride without spot or wrinkle, a glorious church, fulfilling the purpose for which it was established, to preach the Kingdom of God until the earth is filled with the knowledge of the glory of the Lord as the waters cover the sea.

Stan E. DeKoven, Ph.D. MFT,
President, Vision International University

Introduction

In this book, you will read of a conflict that exists between two kingdoms, the Kingdom of Darkness and the Kingdom of Light.

The kingdom that is prevalent and visible to everyone is a world of broken dreams and shattered hopes, a world that is warped and blasted by death and grief. It is the "Kingdom of Darkness," whose lord and prince is Satan. This kingdom is constantly manifesting itself by imposing sickness, disease, poverty, and wars in devastating proportions upon the human race. Yes, it is an obvious Kingdom, with a king, Satan, and thousands of servants (demons and people).

The Kingdom of God coexists in the same world and brings no small stir among some Bible students who want us to believe that the Kingdom of God is not here yet; that the Church will struggle through the so-called Church Age, barely able to persevere against the terrible forces that oppose her. Some teach that the Church will experience the rapture in order to escape the great tribulation. Though this concept is not as prevalent among believers as it used to be, it still exists among many groups today.

My purpose for writing is not to change those who may have a different belief in these areas, but to challenge all who read this material to look prayerfully at the Biblical view of the Kingdom of God, perhaps from a different and larger perspective on the subject than ever before. It is the presence of the Kingdom of God, which brings hope to the world and will triumph over the powers of darkness.

The ancient prophets foresaw these two kingdoms and their parallel existence on the earth. They spoke of the conflict which exists between these two powers a thousand times over. Involved in the conflict is the human race with its fallen nature that can only be reconciled by the cross of Christ. Thus, preaching of "the Gospel of the Kingdom of God" in its fullness is the Father's mandate to the Church.

Finally, my prayer is that you will fully embrace the Kingdom of God, its message, methods and mandate, and that you will take your place in the continuing and forever victory that is in Christ.

Dr. Joseph Thornton

Chapter 1

The Church and The Kingdom

The Church is only different from the Kingdom in that the Church, the "Ecclesia," is the administrative agent of Kingdom affairs. She flows and serves the same purpose as the smaller streams of water contribute to the larger bodies of water. Her theme is redemption. Her purpose is to impact the entire world, and affect the process of history until *"the kingdoms of this world shall become the Kingdom of our Lord and of His Christ." (Revelation 11:15).*

Jesus clearly stated that the Church was to play the role of acting agent, operating in the full authority of Christ. Christ said to the Apostle Peter in Matthew 16:18, *"I give you the keys to the Kingdom whatsoever you loose on earth is loosed in heaven."* Jesus said in Matthew 24:14, *"And this gospel of the Kingdom shall be preached into all the world for a witness to all nations and then the end shall come."*

The Kingdom of God is not merely a collection of religious dogmas, but instead is a biblical truth embodied in the person of Jesus Christ, who He is, and what the Kingdom is all about. Some will say that Babylon represents false religion, and world commerce, and to this I agree. False world religions that represent the harlot woman of the apocalypse are a very real part of the Kingdom of Darkness that the satanic forces rule (Revelation 17:5). John says in the book Revelation, that all earthly governments and kingdoms are fallen (Revelation 14:8).

This has puzzled people for many years, which is "a positive declaration" of a present reality.

In the heart of every true Kingdom child of God, *"Babylon is fallen."* He who sees things that are not as though they were has the authority to speak of the Kingdom as it exists in its present and future states. Some will ask if the Kingdom of God is in the now. If so, why is there not more evidence of this fact? Each time I hear the question, it becomes aware to me that this truth is hard for the natural mind to comprehend, because these two kingdoms parallel each other while existing in the same continuum of time and space. One kingdom brings to bare the forces of darkness in an obvious viciousness, which is meted out in a million different forms. The other kingdom is seemingly not so effective in the work of redemption, because it is spiritually discerned, not being obvious to the natural mind of man. Jesus said that one cannot see the Kingdom until he is born again.

Charles Dickens in *"The Tale of Two Cities"* states, "It was the season of light, it was the season of darkness, it was the spring of hope, it was the winter of despair." This tale of two cities speaks volumes of truth as to the parallel existence of two opposing kingdoms, in which we the people are unintentional participants. While the battle rages on we are caught in "the season of light and the season of darkness." We cannot stand idly by without being drawn into the conflict.

Without the imposing will of Godly men to take a stand against the Kingdom of Darkness, that kingdom will dictate the terms by which men shall live in this present world. Thus, we have two very real kingdoms existing on the earth at the same time.

The children of the Kingdom of God have a very important assignment in that we have been given the keys of the kingdom and are mandated to walk worthy of the "vocation" within which we have been called. The Church has been given the responsibility and authority to administer the affairs of the Kingdom of God. This is our high calling!

Two Worlds Coexist in the Same Continuum of Time and Space

"What you feel when you touch something is not a collision of solids, but of energies in tune in harmony with one another.

"If it were possible to somehow alter the basic nature of the frequencies of matter, to somehow throw matter out of phase with matter as we know it, another world could coexist with this one, "each equally as real as the other," with its own flowers, trees, and people. This world might simultaneously exists in the same physical space and the same continuum of time as our own world; it would be as "solid," and as real as our world is; yet each world could freely pass through the other without either being aware of the other's existence. Being "shifted" in frequency from our world to the alternate world, one would largely be unaffected by the properties of this one. Properties of radiation, gravity, and tactical response would all be out of phase and pass through each other as clearly as light passed through glass."[1]

Jesus could pass through a wall, walk on water, could be thrown into a furnace and walk out unharmed, without even the smell of smoke on his clothes. The Bible tells us that such a world does exist. A.W. Tozer writes, "A spiritual kingdom lies all about us, enclosing us, embracing us, altogether in reach of our inner selves waiting for us to recognize it. God, Himself, is here waiting for our response to His presence." Having to live by the

five senses, of tasting, smelling, feeling, seeing, and hearing inhibits the human race from being able to comprehend this unseen spiritual kingdom. Therefore, it is no wonder that our Lord said that one had to be born again to see the Kingdom of God.

"He said to them, go into all the world and preach the gospel to all creation. Whoever believes and is baptized will be saved, but whoever does not believe will be condemned." (Mark 16:15-16)

---

[1] A quote from "The Nature and Character of God" by W.A. Pratney

Unless the Kingdom of God, the Church, administers the affairs of the Kingdom in power and demonstration of the Spirit, the Kingdom of Darkness will continue to operate in full strength, deceiving the nations.

THE REAL WORLD HIDDEN FROM NATURAL EYES

"Through faith we understand that the worlds were framed by the Word of God, so that things which are seen were not made of things which do appear." (Hebrews 11:3)

"While we look not at things which are seen, but at the things which are not seen; for the things which are seen are temporal; but the things which are not seen are eternal." (II Corinthians 4:18)

How can a world of people be able to comprehend this wonderful truth when they have been taught all their lives that the real things of life are physical and material, and that they should be grasped after and that the accumulation of things is what life is all about?

The writer is saying that the real unseen world is all about us and that all material things get their substance from that world.

It is from the unseen world that we draw from spiritually. To bring the "influence" of this unseen world to bear on the visible world is our mandate. To preach the Gospel of the Kingdom of God, knowing that there is an "ever present and all powerful" unseen realm about us should lead us to a deeper commitment to righteousness and service in our Christian walk. The purpose of this revelation is not to lead us into mindless speculation of future events; nor is it to cause us to fear, but to live in constant hope of our Lord's return.

Our hope for the Kingdom of God to win over the Kingdom of Darkness, lies not in military might, but in the redemptive work of Christ wrought at Calvary, which is the fulfillment of the Abrahamic Covenant, in which God's ultimate purpose is revealed. God said, *"Through your seed shall all the families of the earth shall be blessed."* Christ is the perfected seed of Abraham, as Paul the Apostle stated in Galatians 3:16.

"Thy Kingdom is an everlasting Kingdom and Thy dominion throughout all generations." (Psalm 145:13)

"For unto us a child is born, unto us a son is given; and the government shall be upon His shoulders; and His name shall be

called wonderful, Counselor, the Mighty God, the Everlasting Father, the Prince of Peace." (Isaiah 9:6) [2]

There is nothing to work for outside of the Kingdom of God, for all aspects of the Kingdom of Darkness are no more and no less than an inflated deception perpetrated by demonic inspiration, which is destined to come to an end. Our Lord said, *"And from the days of John the Baptist until now, the Kingdom of Heaven (God) suffers violence and the violent take it by force." (Matthew 11:13).* And again, Jesus said *"the law and the prophets were until John; since that time the Kingdom of God is preached and every man presses into it." (Luke 16:16)*

There is no move of God without men of God.

---

[2] Government – to prevail; have power, as a Prince. Strong's Exhaustive Concordance #8280

Chapter 2

The Kingdoms of this World as Foreseen by the Prophet Daniel

BIBLICAL WORLD VIEW

"Your Majesty looked, and there before you stood a large statue – an enormous, dazzling statue, awesome in appearance; the head of the statue was made of pure gold, its chest and arms of silver, its belly and thighs of bronze, its legs of iron, its feet partly of iron and partly of baked clay." (Daniel 2:31-33)

This is the prophecy in historical time where one will determine the understanding of the Kingdom of God.

Daniel tells the king in his dream that he saw "a stone cutout without hands, which smote the image upon his feet, broke the iron and clay to pieces, crushed them until they were carried away by the wind like chaff from a summer threshing floor, and no place was found for them, and the stone became a great mountain that filled the whole earth."

"And wherever the children of men dwell, the beast of the field, and the fowls of the heaven have been given into thy hand, and has made the ruler over all them. Thou art this head of gold." (Daniel 2:38)

Most Biblical historians agree that the Babylon Kingdom, represented by gold, over which Nebuchadnezzar reigned ended about 538 B.C. and was replaced by the Medo-Persian kingdom, represented by silver, described in Daniel 5:28, which ended about 330-340 B.C. In time, this kingdom was replaced by the

Grecian kingdom, represented by brass, which is outlined in Daniel 8:21, which ended about 62 B.C. The Grecian kingdom was replaced by the Roman kingdom, which was represented by iron and clay, which began to weaken under the powerful preaching of the Gospel of the Kingdom of God, during the short earthly reign of our Lord, and the early apostolic church. After the last of the three world kingdoms, it is easy to overlook the Stone Mountain kingdom which relates to the first advent of Christ and the establishing the Gospel of the Kingdom. Many church historians teach that the Roman kingdom (iron and clay) continues to exist up to this present time, and that the Papal system of the Roman Catholic Church headquartered in Rome, descended from that kingdom and is its present representative.

It is my desire to stay away from endless speculation and to state my interest in this Stone (rock) kingdom, a thirst that can only be satisfied by pressing on, and into, all that God intends for His Kingdom people to see and experience.

Preaching the Kingdom of God is central to world evangelism. The Church is an extension of the Abrahamic Covenant.

Genesis 12:3 "all the families of the earth shall be blessed." In Hebrew, the word families can mean a particular family but basically it means nations, in the Greek, nations is "ethnos" from which we get the word "ethnic" or "ethnicity."

"And you are heirs of the prophets and of the covenant God made with your fathers. He said to Abraham, 'Through your offspring all peoples on earth will be blessed." (Acts 3:25)

"If you belong to Christ, then you are Abraham's seed, and heirs according to the promise." (Galatians 3:29)

Peter reminds the Jewish leaders that the Abrahamic Covenant promises were never intended to relate to, or be limited to, Jewish bloodline but to all ethnic groups.

THE KINGDOM OF GOD – A GROWING KINGDOM
THE KINGDOM OF DARKNESS – A DIMINISHING KINGDOM

"And in the days of these kings shall the God of heaven set up a Kingdom, which will never be destroyed and the Kingdom shall not be left to other people, but it shall break in pieces and consume all these kingdoms, and it shall stand forever." (Daniel 2:44)

The ancient prophet Daniel, while interpreting King Nebuchadnezzar's dream of the "graven image," gives a very detailed account in vision form, of these two opposing kingdoms, which was represented by the Babylonian kingdom, and all succeeding earthly kingdoms. Here is a picture of a growing expanding kingdom, the stone that smote the image became a great mountain that filled the whole earth, in which we see the Kingdom of God (the stone kingdoms) crushing all other kingdoms and filling the entire earth.

In trying to put together a picture of the growing expanding Kingdom of God, one could hardly escape having to give a very limited overview of the Book of Revelation, for therein we find the most positive and exciting message of the Kingdom.

The apocalypse provides a clear picture of the raging conflict that exists between the two worlds. The Kingdom of Darkness, and the Kingdom of Light, with the battle lines clearly drawn, always showing the Kingdom of God reigns in righteousness, and the redemptive work of Christ continues to unfold in the midst of conflict. The Kingdom of Darkness works havoc and devastation but finally goes down in utter defeat.

"And there followed another angel saying, Babylon is fallen, is fallen, and that great city, because she made all nations drink the wine of the wrath of her fornication." (Revelation 14:8)

"And he cried mightily with a strong voice saying, Babylon the great is fallen, is fallen, and is become the habitation of devils, and the hold of every foul spirit, and a cage of every unclean and hateful bird." (Revelation 18:2)

We must lose our timidity about the Book of Revelation, with all its strange symbols, and accept the book for what it is; a book that records the Revelation of Jesus Christ. Then one is able to see truth from a different perspective. The Book of Revelation contains many symbolic pictures of this great conflict in three aspects: 1) a triumphant Christ, 2) a victorious Church, 3) a defeated beast system as opposed to the Book being about the antichrist, the mark of the beast, and the harlot church, which are interjections of truth in the mainstream of the whole picture.

Many books have been written about the "mark of the beast" but there is definitely something missing in most of them and in each case, the mark of the beast is imposed upon the peoples. *"...no buying or selling without having received the mark." (Revelation 13:17)*

"Then I saw another angel coming up from the east, having the seal of the living God. He called out in a loud voice to the four angels who had been given power to harm the land and the sea..." (Revelation 7:2)

The concept of not being able to buy or sell without a number. We have overlooked the idea that even now we cannot buy or sell without a mark i.e. social security number, credit card number, etc.

The Lord has a contingent of souls upon whom the mark of the beast is ineffective. For example, in chapter 13, where the mark of the beast is imposed many fail to show in their writings that God has a contingent of souls, i.e. 144,000, who had the name of the Lamb and His father written on their foreheads. These 144,000 represent 12,000, from each of the twelve tribes of Israel, which is a symbolic number. The number twelve stands for government, thus a divine governmental body who has the seal of God upon their foreheads. (Revelation 14:1)

In Revelation 15:2, John lists another group of saints who were victorious over the Beast and were singing the song of "Moses and the Lamb." Again, in Revelation 19, John says that the beast, the kings, and their armies, were assembled to make war with the Lamb, and the Beast was seized with him, the false prophet, and they were thrown into the lake of fire. Revelation 24 lists a group who had not received the mark of the beast. Much more is said about the "mark of the King" than is said about the "mark of the beast."

The Book of Revelation is an unfolding story about a growing, expanding Kingdom. The truth found in these lines offer the believer a challenging alternative to the modern "doomsday" predictions and dispensational teaching that are so prevalent in the Body of Christ.

The prayer of Jesus "Thy Kingdom come" is not some sort of wishful thinking, but a stated fact. As we go through these pages together, my prayer is that the "reader might be challenged each time he or she views the message of the Kingdom of God. To take up the torch of the "Gospel of the Kingdom," and help spread the Good News of the Gospel, until "the Tree of Life, with her twelve kinds of fruit and her healing leaves have brought "healing to all nations." We see the King of kings ruling the entire world through divine government having restored full dominion over all earthly kingdoms.

Chapter 3

The Kingdom of God Defined

Jesus provided no detailed definition of the Kingdom of God. He stated in Matthew 13 that the Kingdom of God "is like unto, wheat, tares, mustard seed, leaven, hidden treasure, and a pearl of great price."

The word "kingdom" is capable of three different meanings: 1) The realms over which a monarch reigns, 2) The people over whom he reigns, 3) The actual rule or reign itself.[3]

WHAT IS THE KINGDOM OF GOD

It is the overall coverage of all that is contained in the heart and mind of God. The Kingdom of God is an extension of the rule of God in the earth.

It is the territory or an area in which a king rules and reigns. It is a sphere in which one holds a preeminent position; a domain or territory over which dominion is exercised. Jesus exercised this dominion during His earthly ministry.

It is an existing righteousness that can be enjoyed by all born again believers. It is a "now" experience and Satan can do nothing to mar its effectiveness in lives of believers.

Jesus is Lord and King over the domain. The Kingdom of God is not just everywhere in general. She can be found operating in local churches, those that are administrating Kingdom affairs through apostolic order, i.e. the five-fold, gift ministry.

It is a theocracy; a government that is God Ruled. The word theocracy comes from two Greek words.

---

[3] New Concept Bible Dictionary of Zondervan Publishing House

- theos – God, Divinity
- krated – to have power; to be chief; to be master of; to rule; to get possession of, to take hold of; to hold in the hand; to keep carefully and faithfully; to continue to hold.[4]

The Kingdom of God is sometimes referred in scripture as "the people of the Kingdom."

"And has made us unto our God, kings and priests; and we shall reign on the earth." (Revelation 5:10)

Here we see the redeemed as a Kingdom because they share in His reign. This appears again in Revelation 1:6, *"and has made us kings and priests unto God, and His Father; to Him be glory and dominion forever and ever."*

The Kingdom of God is the realm in which God's reign is experienced. This realm is both present and future. *"It is a realm which men enter into with violent determination." (Luke 16:16). "Verily I say unto you among them that are born of women there has not risen a greater than John the Baptist; not withstanding he that is least in the Kingdom of Heaven is greater than he." (Matthew 11:11).* So great are the blessings of God's Kingdom in that the least among us who are born again from above are greater than John the Baptist.

"Who has delivered us from the power of darkness, and has translated us into the Kingdom of His dear Son." (Colossians 1:13). In our study so far, we have seen that the Kingdom of God is a present realm in which men enjoy the blessing of God's rule.

Only those who receive the Kingdom of God will accept God's rule in their lives. *"Verily I say unto you, who shall not receive the Kingdom of God as a little child, he shall not enter therein." (Mark 10:15).* Thus, becoming like a little child, we seek God's Kingdom

---

[4] Thayer's Greek English Lexicon

of righteousness, while asking God to rule in our lives. (Matthew 6:33). It is a fact that a child's growth depends on his complete trust in his parents. He has no ability to direct any part of his life, his development depends on the total trust in his parents. Of course, becoming as a child in the Kingdom does not mean that one must go around acting like a child.

God's Kingdom is not merely an abstract rule. The Kingdom is God's rule, dynamically active, is defeating evil and redeeming sinners.

"For as in Adam all die, so in Christ all will be made alive. But each in turn: Christ, the first fruits; then, when he comes, those who belong to him. Then the end will come, when he hands over the kingdom to God the Father after he has destroyed all dominion, authority and power. For he must reign until he has put all his enemies under his feet. The last enemy to be destroyed is death. For he has put everything under his feet. Now when it says that "everything" has been put under him, it is clear that this does not include God himself, who put everything under Christ. When he has done this, then the Son himself will be made subject to him who put everything under him, so that God may be all in all." (I Corinthians 15:22-28)

Here we see the finality of the redemptive work of Christ through the cross. This expresses what the final outcome is going to be. We all died in Adam, but are made alive in Christ, consummating in the total triumphant victory over death. In the Kingdom of God is the revealed purpose and will of God. It is also the desire and pleasure of God. It is a present reality.

SCRIPTURES THAT REVEAL JESUS TO BE LORD AND KING

OLD TESTAMENT

"Hearken unto the voice of my cry, my King, and my God: for unto you will I pray." (Psalm 5:2)

"For unto us a child is born, unto us a son is given: and the government shall be upon his shoulder: and his name shall be called Wonderful, Counselor, The mighty God, The everlasting Father, The Prince of Peace." (Isaiah 9:6)

"Rejoice greatly, O daughter of Zion; shout, O daughter of Jerusalem: behold, thy King cometh unto thee: he is just, and having salvation; lowly, and riding upon an ass, and upon a colt the foal of an ass." (Zechariah 9:9)

"And when thy days be fulfilled, and thou shalt sleep with thy fathers, I will set up thy seed after thee, which shall proceed out of thy bowels, and I will establish his kingdom." (II Samuel 7:12)

NEW TESTAMENT

"Now unto the King eternal, immortal, invisible, the only wise God, be honour and glory forever and ever. Amen." (I Timothy 1:17)
"Which in his times he shall shew, who is the blessed and only Potentate, the King of kings, and Lord of lords." (I Timothy 6:15)
"And from Jesus Christ, who is the faithful witness, and the first begotten of the dead, and the prince of the kings of the earth. Unto him that loved us, and washed us from our sins in his own blood." (Revelation 1:5)

"These shall make war with the Lamb, and the Lamb shall overcome them: for he is Lord of lords, and King of kings: and they that are with him are called, and chosen, and faithful." (Revelation. 17:14)

"And he hath on his vesture and on his thigh a name written, KING OF KINGS, AND LORD OF LORDS." (Revelation. 19:16)
"And when they had this done, they enclosed a great multitude of fishes: and their net broke." (Luke 5:6)

"Until I make thy foes thy footstool. Therefore let all the house of Israel know assuredly, that God hath made that same Jesus, whom ye have crucified, both Lord and Christ." (Acts 2:36)

"Whom Jason hath received: and these all do contrary to the decrees of Caesar, saying that there is another king, one Jesus." (Acts 17:7)

"But to us there is but one God, the Father, of whom are all things, and we in him; and one Lord Jesus Christ, by whom are all things, and we by him." (I Corinthians 8:6)

"Nathanael answered and saith unto him, Rabbi, thou art the Son of God; thou art the King of Israel." (John 1:49)

"Jesus answered, My kingdom is not of this world: if my kingdom were of this world, then would my servants fight, that I should not be delivered to the Jews: but now is my kingdom not from hence." (John 18:36)

"For to this end Christ both died, and rose, and revived, that he might be Lord both of the dead and living." (Romans 14:9)

"That which was from the beginning, which we have heard, which we have seen with our eyes, which we have looked upon, and our hands have handled, of the Word of life; (For the life was manifested, and we have seen it, and bear witness, and shew unto you that eternal life, which was with the Father, and was manifested unto us;) That which we have seen and heard declare we unto you, that ye also may have fellowship with us: and truly our fellowship is with the Father, and with his Son Jesus Christ. And these things write we unto you, that your joy may be full." (I John 1:1-4)

THE ETERNAL EXISTENCE TO THE KINGDOM OF GOD

The Kingdom of God is from eternity to eternity. There can be no kingdom without a king. So tell me how long the King has been in existence and I will tell you how long the Kingdom has been in existence. According to Psalm 103:19, 145:10; Luke 1:31-33; Isaiah 9:6; II Peter 1:11, the Kingdom is an everlasting Kingdom.

Is there further revelation to come concerning the Kingdom of God? The answer is yes. Every revelation and doctrine that is of God is always seen from three perspectives – the past, present, and future.

THE KINGDOM OF GOD MANIFESTED

Manifestation: Strong's Exhaustive Concordance #602 – to bring forth; bring to light; to be clearly seen, to understand; uncover, disclosure; appearing, coming; to be revealed.

Kingdom: king with a domain; Jesus is King now over His Kingdom

The four manifestations of the Kingdom of God as revealed through the four "**P**"s:

- A **picture** of the Kingdom
- A **purpose** of the Kingdom
- A **person** of the Kingdom
- A **perpetuation** of the Kingdom

The three cardinal virtues of the Kingdom of God are **faith, hope, and love**. Bible students know quite well that one sees, enters, and experiences the Kingdom of God through faith and the new birth.

"For by grace you have been saved through faith; and that not of yourselves, it is the gift of God." (Ephesians 2:8)

"Jesus answered and said unto them, truly, truly I say unto you, unless one is born again he cannot see the Kingdom of God." (John 3:3)

The word "see" in the Greek has broader meaning than just to be able to see something with the natural eye. In the Greek language the meaning is to "behold," "perceive," "to know," "to understand." It requires faith for one to comprehend the Kingdom however faith must be interwoven with the virtues of hope and love.

"In Christ Jesus neither circumcision nor uncircumcision has any value. The only thing that counts is faith expressing itself through love." (Galatians 5:6)

"And now these three remain: faith, hope and love. But the greatest of these is love." (I Corinthians 13:13)

"And hope does not put us to shame, because God's love has been poured out into our hearts through the Holy Spirit, who has been given to us." (Romans 5:5)

The apostle says that "hope does not disappoint." Hope means to anticipate, with pleasure, expectation, and confidence. So to see the Kingdom means that one is living in persistent faith, hope, and love. These virtues are the very "fabric" of the Pauline epistles.

The Kingdom of God cannot be seen or comprehended by mere human observation; this is one reason carnal-minded men have such a struggle when it comes to understanding Kingdom principles.

"Once, on being asked by the Pharisees when the kingdom of God would come, Jesus replied, 'The coming of the kingdom of God is not something that can be observed, or will people say, 'Here it is,' or 'There it is,' because the kingdom of God is in your midst." (Luke 17:20-21)

The signs of which Jesus spoke of in Matthew 12:38-39, are not to be confused with those spoken of in Mark 16:17. Regardless of whether or not one sees the Kingdom of God, the Kingdom is now in your midst. Jesus is saying that wherever the King is, so also is the Kingdom. Just as He told Nicodemus in John 3, you cannot see the Kingdom of God unless you are born again.

Is it not true that many people have the same problem when it comes to locating the Kingdom of God? May the Spirit of revelation so illuminate our minds as to see that the Kingdom of God is now. Jesus is not saying that the Kingdom of God cannot be seen at all, instead, He is saying that it is seen only by the children of the Kingdom and is hidden from carnal or worldly eyes.

The unregenerated heart cannot see the Kingdom of God. The only way one is able to see the Kingdom is when the power of the Kingdom is demonstrated by the power and manifestation of the Holy Spirit.

We see here a principle of the Kingdom that many people do not comprehend. I call it the "principle of spiritual sight" or "seeing spiritually." Jesus is saying that "the world" cannot see the Kingdom because of having unregenerated eyes, and you, His disciples, are able to see; not only the visible aspect of the Kingdom and of Christ, but the results of the Father and the Son coming to abide in you. This is more real than the literal or physical seeing. It is at this point we discover the "age old problem" that has always existed; "having eyes to see but not seeing, ears to hear but not hearing." The world then and now, could not and cannot believe that Jesus restored the Kingdom of God because they were then and now seeing from the wrong perspective.

The Jewish people were looking for a Messianic-Kingdom, with a king similar to the Roman emperors, with an army powerful enough to crush the Roman army. They could not believe that this humble carpenter's son could be such a person. In their eyes, He surely could not carry Messianic-credentials or fulfill their expectations when it came to meeting the qualifications of their Messiah. Trying to see the Kingdom of God with natural, unregenerated eyes is a sure way to miss seeing it at all.

KINGDOM OF GOD BUSINESS
VS
KINGDOM OF DARKNESS BUSINESS

"But I tell you, do not resist an evil person. If anyone slaps you on the right cheek, turn to them the other cheek also." (Matthew 5:39)

The way business is conducted in the Kingdom of God is different than the way the world conducts business. The accumulation of things is the goal of the world, but not in the Kingdom of God.

Kingdom of God business is conducted in a way that appears to be anti-principle, according to the way the Kingdom of Darkness operates.

- The Kingdom of Darkness says, "crush your enemies," The Kingdom of God says, "love you enemies and pray for those who spitefully use you."
- The Kingdom of Darkness says, "fight back when someone smites you," the Kingdom of God says, "turn the other cheek when someone smites you."
- The Kingdom of Darkness only goes one mile, and only does that when it is profitable to do so. The Kingdom of God says go the first mile because it is right to do so, go the second mile because of love. In Matthew 5:14, a Jew was required by Roman law to carry a Roman soldier's bag for him.
- The Kingdom of Darkness says, "Get to the top, even if you have to use other people as stepping stones in order to do so." The Kingdom of God says, "Go down" and let God raise you up in His time. For those who exalt themselves will be humbled, and those who humble themselves will be exalted."

The Kingdom of God says, "the first shall be last, the last shall first." As far as the world is concerned, the Kingdom of God is an "upside-down kingdom." One surrenders his rights of ownership when he enters the Kingdom of God. The children of the Kingdom own nothing, yet possess all things. The people of the world are out "to own it all," but how free from encumbrance is a person who has surrendered his rights of ownership to Christ.

"Sorrowful, yet always rejoicing; poor, yet making many rich; having nothing, and yet possessing everything." (II Corinthians 6:10)

Another spiritual principle taught in Scripture is called the "principle of ownership." It seems as though the Jewish people believed that they had the one and only franchise to the Kingdom of God with exclusive rights to the privileges thereof.

"Here there is no Gentile or Jew, circumcised or uncircumcised, barbarian, Scythian, slave or free, but Christ is all, and is in all." (Colossians 3:11)

Here the apostle is saying there was to be a conglomerate of ethnic groups that make up the Kingdom, and that it is not an exclusive Jewish club.

"But the subjects of the kingdom will be thrown outside, into the darkness, where there will be weeping and gnashing of teeth." (Matthew 8:12)

Again, the Lord is saying that there was to be a gathering of ethnic groups that would make up the Kingdom which is not for Jews alone. To illustrate the point, He went on to say that the people of the Kingdom, meaning the Jewish people, who had enjoyed the exclusive privileges and rights of the Kingdom would be cast out of the Kingdom. He is saying that He is the King, and that He is owner of the domain of His Kingdom. It would be well to take note that nowhere in Scripture is the Kingdom of God ever called the Kingdom of man. It is not called the Jewish kingdom, neither is it called a Gentile kingdom - it is called the Kingdom of God.

"He came to his own, but his own did not receive him. Yet to all who did receive him, to those who believed in his name, he gave the right to become children of God." (John 1:11-12)

The scripture is quite clear here. The statement "He came to His own" means that He came first to old Israel. "His own received Him not", He is saying that the ritualistic Mosaic system did not receive Him. The Lord went on to say, "but as many as received Him, He gave the right to become children of God."

"For if God did not spare the natural branches, neither will He spare you." (Romans 11:21). Paul tells us to beware and to learn a lesson about the cutting off of the natural branches. He is basically

saying the same thing as Jesus said in Matthew 8, in reference to "the children being cast out of the Kingdom." It is the vine that bears the branches, the branches do not bear the vine. Christ being the vine.

The Mosaic Law ended in Christ and its order of service came to an end. One could not honestly read the New Testament epistles without realizing that the order of the law ceased; also that there is no one particular race of people today that have exclusive rights to the Kingdom of God above and beyond any other. It is important for the student of the Word to know that old Mosaic order of worship and approach to God will never be reinstated again, for Jesus was the perfect sacrifice that met every requirement of the law. Christ fulfilled all 330 plus Messianic prophecies that were spoken by the Old Testament prophets. Though there might be a time when the Jewish people will try to reinstate the Mosaic ritual of service, it will have nothing to do with the Kingdom of God.

"For I am not ashamed of the gospel for it the power of God unto salvation to everyone who believes, to Jew first and also to the Greek." (Romans 1:16). It is quite clear that the "good news" of the Gospel of Christ has come first to the Jewish people, secondly to the Gentiles. It is to be understood that the word "Gentile" means, "unconverted heathen nations."

"When the Jews saw the crowds, they were filled with jealousy. They began to contradict what Paul was saying and heaped abuse on him. Then Paul and Barnabas answered them boldly: "We have to speak the word of God to you first. Since you reject it and do not consider yourselves worthy of eternal life, we now turn to the Gentiles." (Acts 13:45-46)

Here we see Christ as King of kings and Lord of lords ruling over His Kingdom. Paul and Barnabas were fulfilling a 600-year-old prophecy which was spoken by the prophet Isaiah. In Isaiah 42:6; the prophet says that the Lord is "taking a people who were not a people to make up a remnant called the elect of God." All ethnic groups can rejoice over the fact that all peoples are children of the Abrahamic Covenant by faith. (Isaiah 55:5)

"Therefore, since we are receiving a kingdom that cannot be shaken, let us be thankful, and so worship God acceptably with reverence and awe." (Hebrews 12:28).

The word "kingdom" here, just as in other passages of scripture, means the same "a foundation of power and sovereign rule," a king with a domain. I will paraphrase, "you have received the rule of God, the Sovereign One." The writer did not say you are going to receive a kingdom in the future, instead, he said you have received the Kingdom. The Kingdom of God is spoken of as being present now. I am speaking of a tangible, vital, living, pulsating reality; a Kingdom of righteousness, peace, and joy in the Holy Spirit – now.

FELLOWSHIP WITH CHRIST AT THE LORD'S TABLE
A KINGDOM PRIVILEGE

"And he said to them, "I have eagerly desired to eat this Passover with you before I suffer. For I tell you, I will not eat it again until it finds fulfillment in the kingdom of God." (Luke 22:15-16)

It is quite evident that the eating of the Passover was a special occasion to Jesus because it was the last time He would do so *"until it be fulfilled in the Kingdom of God."* Therefore, God's intent for the Lord's Supper (which is called communion by many), is to be an expression of God's Kingdom on earth. Jesus was not saying that He would partake with His disciples upon His second, and final return. He said, *"I will partake when the Kingdom of God is come."*

How much greater would be the blessing at the communion table if the Body of Christ really believed that Christ was present each time we gather together to partake of the Lord's Supper. Would there not be greater forgiveness, healing, and restoration?

It is quite possible that the Body of Christ, as a whole, has lost the true meaning of fellowship at the Lord's Supper. What joy divine would be experienced if the Church of Christ had the full revelation of Christ's presence at the table?

"And I appoint unto you a kingdom, as my Father hath appointed unto me." (Luke 22:2)

The Kingdom is appointed by God, so being allowed to eat and drink at the table of the Lord in His Kingdom is a special privilege. All believers should conduct themselves in a way that will bring honor to this great event.

40

Chapter 4

Lordship in the Kingdom

"But you are not to be like that. Instead, the greatest among you should be like the youngest, and the one who rules like the one who serves." (Luke 22:26)

"For I think that God has exhibited us apostles as last of all, like men sentenced to death, because we have become a spectacle to the world, to angels, and to men." (I Corinthians 4:9)

WHOSE RIGHT IT IS TO RULE IN THE KINGDOM

The apostle makes it emphatically clear that leaders in the Kingdom have to surrender their rights in order to be led by the Holy Spirit, ministering to others even unto death. The apostle might have had in mind, that the one whom God ordained to administer the affairs of the Kingdom could be likened to one that is chained to the oars of a slave ship. Though all on board, including the captain, might be able to abandon the sinking vessel, those who are condemned to die, being chained to the oars could only keep on rowing, setting forth the example, to the total abandonment of the right to ownership. (I Corinthians 4:9)

Jesus said that exercising lordship over the people was a Gentile (heathen) practice, and was not to be done in His Kingdom. He uses an Old Testament expression in v26 concerning "the greatest being as the youngest." Jesus is setting forth a truth found in Genesis 48, where the patriarch Jacob who was moved by the Spirit of God to cross his hands while blessing Joseph's two sons, Ephraim and Manasseh. Instead of giving the birth

right blessing to the elder by placing his right hand upon his head, he placed it upon the younger. The crossing of his hands pointed to the cross of Christ, and the time when the birthright blessing would no longer go to just Old Israel, but to all children of faith. (Genesis 48:12-13)

It is my belief that "the greatest among them" (Luke 22) was in reference to Old Israel, at least up until the time of Christ, but Christ had ushered in the Kingdom, He is saying that the first (Old Israel) shall be last. And that the children who believe the message of reconciliation i.e. all ethnic groups, shall be first. Christ is also saying that "serving" is a vital ingredient of the Kingdom of God. It is a natural, Christ-like nature that's inherent in the people of the Kingdom.

The Kingdom that the Lord offered Nicodemus in John 3 was not just an emotionally charged feeling, nor a "goose bump" religious experience that would come and go with the changing of time and circumstance. Instead, He offered him an inner kingdom of righteousness, peace, and joy in the Holy Spirit, now, and not just to be experienced at some future date. Jesus said that the greatest among us were to become servants to all. Peter warned that God's ministers were not to be "lords" over God's heritage, but we were to be examples to the flock. (I Peter 5:3)

Principles of True Shepherding

Some spiritual leaders have missed God in the area of shepherding. We have seen some driving the sheep, rather than leading them besides still waters.

"And when he puts forth his own sheep, he goes before them, and the sheep follow him: for they know his voice" (John 10:4)

A "pastor' is a shepherd. He is a leader, not a dictator.

"Jesus answered them, and said, My doctrine is not mine, but his that sent me, "He that speaks of himself seeks his own glory: but he that seeks his glory that sent him, the same is true, and no unrighteousness is in him." (John 7:16-18)

Two Classes of Leaders
Servant Leaders and Self-Serving Leaders

Christ, the servant leader is an example for all ministers to follow.

"I can do nothing on My own initiative. As I hear, I judge; and My judgment is just, because I do not seek My own will, but the will of Him who sent Me. If I alone testify about Myself, My testimony is not true." (John 5:30:31)

Jesus is the model minister. What can the shepherd leaders do to set the example that He laid out for us? The key word is "excellence" in serving which has to do with attitude.

"And while being reviled, He did not revile in return; while suffering, He uttered no threats, but kept entrusting Himself to Him who judges righteously." (I Peter 2:23)

"He made Himself of no reputation but emptied Himself, taking the form of a bond-servant, and being made in the likeness of men." (Philippians 2:7)

For the ecclesia, "the called-out ones," to be able to express Christ to the world is to be excellent in serving. A true shepherd will get involved in every aspect of administering the affairs of the Kingdom.

Physical Aspect of Serving

The five-fold ministry leaders of the New Testament church did not stay in the comfort of the house while expecting others to serve them. They stayed on call; they are not driven men. Neither are they hirelings, one who fleece the sheep. A hireling is one who flees when he sees the wolf coming.

Spiritual Aspect of Serving in the Kingdom

Serving in the kingdom has to do with one's destiny in Christian service in three areas:

- relationship with God
- the family unit
- ministry in the local Body of Christ – all which is an ongoing labor of love

To be pleasing to the Father "teamwork" in ministry is required. We are fellow workers and there is to be "equal accountability" required in every aspect of responsibility, from preaching to dishwashing, and in the area of apostolic succession relating to the impartation and transferal of authority to the next generation of leaders. For there to be succession of leadership in the Kingdom, there must be first an impartation in the areas of call, vision, and faithful to Kingdom vision.

Moving from one level of responsibility to another is never easy. Realignments and readjustments are imperative if we are to improve the level of excellence in serving. When greater performance is required, it is not meant for punishment; rather it is meant for the advancement of the Kingdom.

THE SPIRITUAL

Our destiny is in family, as well as ministers in the Kingdom.

*"A Father to the fatherless, a judge and protector of the widows is God in His holy habitation. God places the **solitary** in families and gives the desolate a home in which to dwell, He leads the prisoners out to prosperity; but the rebellious dwell in a parched land" (Psalm 68:5-6)*

"Solitary" (a sacredness; aloneness) is a special chamber in the heart of the Father that is reserved just for families. Father God came to planet earth because He wanted fellowship with sons and daughters. A true shepherd understands this and develops a "father's love" for family life.

Proper Priorities in the Dynamics of Kingdom Living

- God
- Family
- Body of Christ
- Church Life

When building ones' private agenda, temples or castles; leaders must set examples in caring for their families. It is not pleasing to the Lord when ministers sacrifice their own families in order to minister to the Body of Christ.

"The LORD appeared to Abram and said, "To your descendants I will give this land." So he built an altar there to the LORD who had appeared to him" (Genesis 12:7)

"Then Abram moved his tent and came and dwelt by the oaks of Mamre, which are in Hebron, and there he built an altar to the LORD." (Genesis 13:18)

"Then they came to the place of which God had told him; and Abraham built the altar there and arranged the wood, and bound his son Isaac and laid him on the altar, on top of the wood." (Genesis 22:9)

Each time God appeared to Abraham, and gave him a special assignment, he built an altar to the Lord as opposed to other men, which God may have appeared with a special visitation but refused to build an altar unto the Lord, but rather build themselves a name. Abraham's response to the presence of God was to surrender his right of ownership, and was willing to sacrifice his son Isaac, thus becoming the only perfect type of Father God in the Old Testament.

Abraham birthed his son Isaac; his son Isaac birthed Jacob; Jacob gave birth to the twelve tribes of Israel, which shows the Father's heart and concern for family life. The grace of surrendering one's right to ownership is a principle by which one multiplies and increases in the Kingdom.

Though Jesus never married during his earthly life, he is married now…to the church, the body of Christ, the family of God, the Bride of Christ. He is indeed King, he rules with love, compassion, tenderness and grace and as husband and father in his family, the church.

Chapter 5

The Timing and Birth of a Nation

BRINGING FORTH FRUIT

"Jesus said unto them, "Did you never read in the scriptures, the stone which the builders rejected, the same is become the head cornerstone: this is the Lord's doing, and it is marvelous in our eyes?" (Matthew 21: 42-43)

Jesus states that the Kingdom of God will be taken from old Israel (old Mosaic system) not from the people of Israel, and given to a "nation" that will bring forth fruit.

The Greek word for nation is "ethnos," from which we get our English word "ethnic."[5] The inference is that old Israel sought their justification by works of the law, rejected their Messiah, thus resulting in losing their Messianic Kingdom. The pagan Gentile world so appreciated the gift of grace and righteousness that they were able to inherit the Abrahamic covenant by faith, and brought forth "fruit of the Kingdom."

The Kingdom of God affects every nation, ethnic group, and all life, here and now, is influenced by the Kingdom of God. Its effects go well beyond just the saving of souls. The Kingdom ministers to the family, in the work place, and to every social and economic arena of the world.

The following verses make an emphatic declaration as to the present-tense Kingdom of God.

---

[5] Nation: a race, non-Jewish, pagan, Gentile, heathen nation. Strong's Exhaustive Concordance

"Truly I say to you, this generation will not pass away until all these things take place." (Matthew 24:34)

"And he said to them, "Truly I tell you, some who are standing here will not taste death before they see that the kingdom of God has come with power." (Mark 9:1)

Did Jesus really mean that some of His disciples would live to see the Kingdom of God? Yes, and no amount of theology can make what He said to mean anything else. He ushered in the Kingdom at His coming and some standing there lived to see it.

"After John had been taken into custody, Jesus came in to Galilee, preaching the Gospel of God and saying, the time is fulfilled and the Kingdom of God is at hand; repent and believe the Gospel." (Mark 1:14-15)

"But He said to them, I must preach the Kingdom of God to the other cities also, for I was sent for this purpose." (Luke 4:43)

"And when Jesus saw that He had answered intelligently, He said to him, you are not far from the Kingdom of God. And after that no one would venture to ask Him any more questions" (Mark 12:34)

"And it came about soon afterwards, that He began going about from one city and village to another, proclaiming and preaching the Kingdom of God and the twelve were with Him." (Luke 8:1)

"He sent them to preach the Kingdom of God and to heal the sick." (Luke 9:2)

The message Jesus preached and demonstrated was the Kingdom of God. This is the same message his team (disciples/apostles) preached; the same message we are to preach to see his Kingdom manifested today.

THY KINGDOM IS COME

"Until the day when He was taken up to heaven, after He had by the Holy Spirit given orders to the apostles whom He had chosen. To

these He also presented Himself alive after His suffering, by many convincing proofs, appearing to them over a period of forty days and speaking of the things concerning the kingdom of God." (Acts 1:1-3)

"Then they gathered around him and asked him, "Lord, are you at this time going to restore the kingdom to Israel? He said to them: "It is not for you to know the times or dates the Father has set by his own authority. But you will receive power when the Holy Spirit comes on you; and you will be my witnesses in Jerusalem, and in all Judea and Samaria, and to the ends of the earth." (Acts 1:6-8)

The question here was an obvious one of Jewish thinking, prevalent even in His disciples. Will you restore the Kingdom of God back to Israel at this time? In spite of Jesus' teaching about taking the Kingdom from them and giving it to another nation bearing the fruit thereof, they still believed that God was going to restore old Mosaic order, and set up a Messianic, Jewish kingdom that would rule the entire world.

It is surprising how much this sounds like those who teach that the nation of Israel gets a second chance to recapture the Kingdom. Jesus is saying that when you are baptized with the Holy Spirit, you will know not to ask such a question as, "When will the Kingdom be restored back to Israel?" The Kingdom will never return to the old Mosaic order. The old Mosaic covenant will never be revitalized. Animal sacrifices have been done away with forever. "My blood is to be offered once, and for all, as atonement of your sins and for the entire world." Had they asked the Lord "when will you introduce to us, the Kingdom of God" or "when will you reveal the Kingdom of God to all nations?" His answer would be "the Kingdom of God is among you, go preach it to all nations." You are witnessing the first stage of the Kingdom of God even now, as I speak and you will see the Kingdom of God in your lifetime. You are not to wait until after the rapture and the seven-year great tribulation.

It is better to look unto Jesus, the author and finisher of our faith, than it is to look to an earthly Jerusalem. The Bible says nothing about rebuilding a temple of worship in Jerusalem in our day or in the future. Jesus said that not one stone of the temple would be left standing. He said to the women at the well that true worshipers were not to worship "in this mountain," meaning the mountain where the Samaritans worshipped, "nor yet in Jerusalem" where the Jews worshipped; but that the true worshippers were to worship the Father in "spirit and in truth." "Ye are the temple of the Holy Spirit." We are not to look at an earthly temple of worship made by human hands.

"Do you not know that you are a temple of God and that the Spirit of God dwells in you; if any man destroys the temple of God, God will destroy him, for the temple of God is holy, and that is what you are." (I Corinthian 3:16-17)

"But Solomon built him a house. Howbeit the Most High dwells not in temples made with hands; as says the prophet." (Act 7:47-48)

"God that made the world and all things therein, seeing that he is Lord of heaven and earth, dwells not in temples made with hands." (Acts 17:24)

We are now living in the Kingdom age, made up of Jew and Gentile, as one new man in the earth in an everlasting Kingdom.

THE ABOMINATION OF DESOLATION

"When you see 'the abomination that causes desolation' standing where it does not belong (let the reader understand) then let those who are in Judea flee to the mountains." (Mark 13:14)

Jesus talked to His disciples about the "abomination of desolation," the destruction of Jerusalem, and the end of the age (not the world). He said to His disciples that some of them would live to see this event, referring to the abomination of desolation; and that this would be a sign that they should get out of Jerusalem and Judea before it happened. Great tribulation would begin to fall on that area. He was prophesying the end of an age, a world that was ending," meaning the Old Testament world, while introducing the new that was being ushered in at that present time. (Old Testament world, New Testament world)

The abomination that Jesus spoke of is a thing of the past. To lift it from the past and try to make a future event out of it is pure speculation. There are those who will disagree "doctrinally" with me but we will continue to have fellowship in the Spirit, not controlled by a "disagreeable spirit of strife." The occurrence of the abomination that defiled the sanctuary, which Daniel spoke of, was not a onetime event.

The following is from a book entitled "The Abomination of Desolation" by Evangelist John L. Bray, "In Jewish terminology, an abomination was anything that involved the worship of false gods in sacred places." The Jewish people understood clearly the meaning of the word, "abomination." Yet so many "end time" prophecy preachers have removed it from the past and are making it a thing of the future, as if the "abomination" is some sort of prophetic "end-time" event.

Evangelist John L. Bray goes on to say that, "Antiochus Epiphanes, in December of 168 B.C. profaned the temple with his pagan actions and caused a pig to be barbecued in sacrifice to the god Zeus." Jesus understood full well what it meant. What He was saying about the abomination was in reference to what the prophet Daniel spoke in Daniel 11:31. Thus, when they saw the Roman Governor, Titus, with his Roman armies surrounding Jerusalem, they were to remove themselves from the city. Though the "desecration of the temple" was a literal paganistic happening, it could also be in reference to the lawless one, referring to a "total corrupt" political power, which will make its final evil effort, "to make war with the Lamb and the Lamb will overcome them." (Revelation 17:13-14)

"But I tell you the truth; there are some standing here which shall not taste death until they see the Kingdom of God." (Luke 9:27).

To try to make a past event into a present event sends a confused message to God's people. All students of the Word should keep an open mind in areas of doctrinal teaching about future "end time" events.

The age-old game of speculation goes on and on with many interpretations of when the end will come and when the

Kingdom of God will be restored. My purpose in writing is to encourage the sincere reader of God's Word, that there are some alternatives to look at as opposed to accepting what many have preached as prophecy, concerning "end-time" events. Beware of the game that one must play if we are to keep up with all that is said in the name of "end-time prophecies." We do not want to miss the main event of the Kingdom, which is to preach the Gospel of the Kingdom of God. The Kingdom in all its beauty; living and abiding in each believer while ruling over Satan's domain.

I conclude that Jesus meant what He said concerning, "some standing here shall not taste death until they see the Kingdom of God." He was saying that the Kingdom is **now** and not just some time in the future.

Chapter 6

Two Kingdoms Clash

"Write therefore the things which you have seen, and the things which are, and the things which shall take place after these things." (Revelation 1:19)

John is saying that from the present time and thereafter there would be a demonic force coming against the Church, the likes of which had never been seen before. John knew that our fight is not for victory but that we fight from a place of victory.

John was undoubtedly the only living apostle on whom the Lord could give such a task. He was the last survivor of the twelve, the others had been martyred years prior to this time, and John was a victim of Roman suppression, having been banished to the Isle of Patmos because of his testimony for Jesus Christ. God had raised up John for this momentous task, and brought him into the Kingdom for such a time as this. One had to be able to write from the vantage point of Heaven's perspective in order to carry out such an assignment. He wrote about things of the past, things of the present, and things to come, for one to witness such horrific war he needed to be protected in a safe place.

Just what did John see? One would have to know the history of John's life and ministry, in order to answer the question. He had witnessed the powerful ministry of Jesus Christ, and the forces of hell that relentlessly opposed Him, and finally His resurrection, which caused no small stir among the Jewish religious leaders. John witnessed the outpouring of the Holy Spirit during the Pentecost feast. He saw the birthing of the Church of Jesus Christ which was to become the official voice

and acting agent in charge of the affairs of the Kingdom of God. He had seen, and was active in the spreading of the Gospel, which was preached "to every creature under heaven." (Colossians 1:23) John would witness the old Jewish order being replaced by the Kingdom of God and the destruction of Jerusalem by the Romans in 70 A.D, which was prophesied by the Lord in Matthew 24. He saw the things that were going to take place in the near future, such as the spreading of the Kingdom of God into all areas of planet earth. John knew that the destruction of Jerusalem would end the Jews exclusive rights to relationship with God. Thus, the franchise of the Kingdom was no longer a Jewish one; later it was attested at the great Jerusalem conference in Acts 15, when the Jewish Church was disputing the Gentile Church in saying that in order to be saved one had to be circumcised. The ludicrousness of that requirement was exposed and eliminated.

John had a heavy heart, having the responsibility placed upon him to write the Book of Revelation. He no doubt had to proceed with caution, clearly under the inspiration of the Holy Spirt, for this assignment could not be accomplished by effort of human intelligence. That is why John said, "I was in the Spirit on the Lord's day." Being in the Spirit gave John the distinct and unique advantage, enabling him to accomplish such a fantastic task. How refreshing it would be if today's prophecy preachers, those who feel mandated to spread the Gospel, would be as cautious as John in their writings. It is essential that we do not allow our present world circumstances to dictate how we read and study God's word. We must minister the truth of God's word from the standpoint of "being in the spirit on the Lord's day," seeing things from heaven's perspective, ministering from victory to victory, not from fear of the anti-Christ or the Mark of the Beast. It is time that preachers see things from this perspective and stop trying to outdo one another in predicting end-time events, rapture and the second coming of Christ."

"Therefore I say unto you, the Kingdom of God will be taken away from you, and be given to a nation producing the fruit of it." (Matthew 21:43)

Perhaps the heaviest task that lied upon John's heart was the fact that he had lived to see the Kingdom of God being taken from old Israel and given to another, and now his assignment from God was to write. He no doubt assumed that his fading reputation would get worse because of the feelings of superiority that were prevalent in the Jewish church, which he loved so dearly, knowing that factions of all kinds would arise. John foresaw the Gentile world being converted to Christianity, and so he proceeded to write with caution in the spirit. John knew that the spreading of the Gospel of the Kingdom of God was the fulfillment of the Abrahamic covenant, and that the Gospel was being given to all nations, i.e. ethnic groups.

John also knew that the attacking forces of darkness would not be satisfied with trying to squelch the Jerusalem church, and the immediate surrounding areas only. He knew that the seed of the Kingdom of God had been planted and was springing up to other parts of the world, and that the Kingdom of Darkness would do all in its powers to stamp it out before it became "the full corn in the ear."

Thus, this tired, weary old soldier of the cross was endeavoring to be faithful to his final and last Kingdom assignment before he went home to be with the Lord. He was assigned to write things that he knew would be misinterpreted by many; things a million men would use to twist the Scripture to suit themselves. One can hardly imagine just how heavy his heart was at the thought of

God's people, yet having to undergo more persecution and torture. Had it not been enough, thus far? But no, he knew that the persecution of God's people would last many years; a persecution master minded by satanic strategy would be so severe that one day the persecutors would celebrate that this heretic group of Christians had been wiped out completely. There was a period of time in which Christians would be slaughtered for the testimony of Jesus Christ, many for no other reason than to satisfy the sadistic perversion of Roman emperors. Persecution of the disciples was used by God to scatter believers abroad, thus expanding the church. In spite of the persecution, the church gained momentum. In 70 AD, immediately after the temple was destroyed, persecution continued for over 1,200 years, and continues to this day. Thus, John proceeds to write, in symbolic language, while vividly painting a portrait of a...

- Triumphant King
- Triumphant Kingdom of God
- Defeated Beast System
- Triumphant Church (Revelation 5:10)

We accept the fact that the Kingdom of Darkness and the Kingdom of Light are in total opposition of each other and will be at war until the Kingdom of God is ultimately victorious.

This is a very limited look at the Book of Revelation. However, I will say in conclusion that the Book of Revelation plays a very significant role in the doctrine of the Kingdom of God.

Chapter 7

Four Manifestations of the Kingdom of God

A Divine Portrait of the Kingdom

It is important to know there are many types in the Old Testament that prefigured the coming Kingdom of God, all which play a role in interpreting the Book of Revelation.

First Manifestation – Adam and Eve in the Garden

The first manifestation of the Kingdom of God begins in the Garden of Eden with Adam and Eve. It is here that we get a glimpse of God's design and a clear picture of the Kingdom of God; a transparent relationship which existed between God and man, naked and not ashamed, with man having dominion over all the earth. The Father's intent was that man was to be His Kingdom, subservient partner. The incredible work of creation described in Genesis 1 is staggering to the imagination, to say the least. One cannot enlarge on the Genesis account of creation.

"Out of the ground the LORD God formed every beast of the field and every bird of the sky, and brought them to the man to see what he would call them; and whatever the man called a living creature, that was its name." (Genesis 2:19)

God made man in His own image and likeness. Man was given dominion to "rule over the earth." The ability and privilege to give names to every living creature was no small thing. He not only gave names to the animal world, he also ascribed personality that matched well with the name of each. This alone shows where man stood in his relationship to God. In this we see a picture of what the Kingdom of God was, and how it was to function, then and for all time. Mankind, in full harmony with his Creator is to rule over all living things as well as the earth. This original Edenic experience we will eventually be restored. God's full intent was that Adam be king of the whole world, while replenishing the earth, ruling directly under the Lord of Creation Himself.

"And the man and his wife were both naked and were not ashamed." (Genesis 2:25)

This sets forth what is perhaps the most significant of all God's intent, pertaining to His relationship with Adam and Eve. This is an example of transparency, and innocence that existed between God and Adam and Eve in the first manifestation of the Kingdom. Nothing offensive existed between the Adamic Kingdom and the Kingdom of God before the fall. Adam and Eve lived in perfect innocence and harmony.

If asked, what was lost to man in the Garden, the answer would be, he lost his dominion; a domain over which he was to rule. Adam and Eve were separated from God in their fellowship with Him.

"The Son of Man shall send forth His angels, and shall gather out of His Kingdom, all things that offend, and them which do iniquity." (Matthew 13:41)

God's Purpose for the Original Offense

In the Garden of Eden, God reveals the purpose for the "offense."

"Now the serpent was more subtle than any beast of the field which the Lord God had made. And He said unto the woman, Yea, hath said, ye shall not eat of every tree of the garden?" (Genesis 3:1)

It is hard to imagine that there could be a force found anywhere that was powerful enough to penetrate, infiltrate, and divide the first Kingdom of God. One has to examine the whole plan that the Father had in mind and see, from a larger perspective, what took place in the garden. The question has been asked, 'if God is all powerful, having given full dominion to Adam, why was Satan allowed to enter the garden?"

There seems to be no end to speculation as to why God allowed the serpent to have access to his special creation. We must look further than the garden in order to see the plan that the Father had in mind for His Kingdom. The answer I am sure is too simple to be accepted. If there had been no conflicting force allowed in the garden to oppose man, he would had never developed a will to serve God. He instead would have been like the angels. But thanks be to God for allowing the offense; we have a will to resist Satan. We serve and worship God in spite of tempting and opposing forces that come against us.

The Father of Creation never intended for mankind to be like creatures with no will to choose how they were to worship God. Being able to choose for himself is what makes the Gospel of Christ so effective. The voluntary submitting of one's will to the transforming power of God, while walking as a child of God, causes a debilitating effect on the Kingdom of Darkness.

THE ULTIMATE PURPOSE OF THE FALL MAN

"The LORD God said to the serpent, "Because you have done this, Cursed are you more than all cattle, And more than every beast of the field; On your belly you will go, And dust you will eat All the days of your life; And I will put enmity Between you and the woman, And between your seed and her seed; He shall bruise you on the head, And you shall bruise him on the heel." (Genesis 3:14-15)

The word "enmity" means: to hate as one of an opposing tribe; it means hostility, to be an enemy.

"And I say to thee, that you are Peter, and upon this rock I will build my church, and the gates of hades will not prevail against it." (Matthew 16:18)

The Bible tells us that from the very onset of creation, and in the gospel age that major conflict exists between the Kingdom of God and the Kingdom of Darkness. Jesus said that we have: 1) a "rock," which is the base or foundation, 2) a building, which is the Body of

Christ, 3) a battle (gates of hades). All of which are a part of God's plan.

The Church cannot be built without the battle. The Kingdom of God is under an attack, and always will be, up until the "times of the restitution of all things that the prophets spoke of" (Acts 3:21). Thus, the ultimate purpose of the fall in the garden is for every creature to be reconciled to God by the preaching of the cross. The final "bruising of Satan's head" was accomplished through Christ's death on the cross and the ministry of the Church. God allowed the fall of man. God in His wisdom allowed the opposing forces of hell to make war against His children in order for them to develop a will to resist the powers of darkness. In this is revealed the ultimate purpose for the fall of man.

"And so it is written, that the first man, Adam, was made a living soul, the last Adam was made a quickening spirit." (1 Corinthians 15:45)

A unique relationship exists between what Jesus said to Peter in Matthew 16:18, *"Upon this rock I will build my church,"* and what Paul said in I Corinthians 15:45. Just as Adam was given dominion over "all things," so Christ has been given dominion over all things. The "Head bruiser, Christ," is come to bruise the head of the serpent, and to take back the authority and dominion that Adam abdicated when he rebelled against God in the garden. Christ has passed His dominion to the church. Thus, the Edenic scene was a prophetic promise that the Kingdom of God would be restored.

One could say that Adam and Eve, in the garden, provides a "panoramic view of the Kingdom of God, representing God's intended purpose for the earth, then God must have lost not being wise, not having power enough to guard against intrusions that the Serpent was allowed to make. Could this not happen again and cause God's children to make a total failure of their walk with Christ? There is only one answer to such speculation; the Lord of Creation did not fail. Neither was His purpose thwarted. For as devastating as it might appear, God had a much higher purpose in mind for His Kingdom than could ever have come to fruition or expressed in the Garden of Eden.

Even though the Edenic scene was a manifestation of the Kingdom of God on the Earth, it was only a single photo in comparison to the eventual restoration of the Kingdom of God. Thus, the first manifestation of the Kingdom of God in the garden provides a glimpse of what the Kingdom is supposed to be.

SECOND MANIFESTATION - ABRAHAM

"And the Lord appeared to Abram and said, 'unto thy seed will I give this land', and their he built an altar unto the Lord who appeared unto him" (Genesis 12:7)

In Abraham is revealed the purpose for the Kingdom of God. One cannot build a house and expect it to stand the test of storms and time unless it is built on a solid foundation. A rock represents the scriptural principle of right building which is to be applied in every area of teaching about the Kingdom of God, especially in areas that we build our eternal hope upon.

"And the scripture, foreseeing that God would justify the heathen through faith, preached before the gospel unto Abraham, saying in thee shall all nations be blessed." (Galatians 3:8).

The very seed of the Gospel of the Kingdom of God was found in Abraham. One does not build upon the New Testament alone; there is such a marvelous "meshing together" of the old and new covenants, a great part of the whole picture is lost when one lays aside any part the Old Testament.

Dr. Leonard Coote taught young ministers, "The Old Testament is the **acorn** from which came the New Testament **oak**." There would be no oak without there being an acorn. My advice to any and all students of the Word is that you study both the Old and New Covenants. The Old Testament shows us the altars and foundation of God. The New Testament shows the Temple of God ("no ye not that you are the temple of God, for God dwells not in temples made with hands.")

When one fails to realize that the Gospel originated in Abraham long before Christ, one will most likely not be able to see nor understand much about the Kingdom of God. In Abraham is a prophetic revelation that foretells the very heart of the Father. His desire is to see His Kingdom covering the whole world. One should think of Abraham in larger terms than just the fact that he was a great man of faith. Think of him in terms of God's divine and ultimate purpose for the Kingdom of God. In Abraham is the unconditional covenant and purpose of God and man.

"And I will make my covenant between Me and thee, and will multiply thee exceedingly. And Abraham fell on his face; and God talked with him, saying... as for me, behold My covenant is with thee, and you shall be the father of many nations." (Genesis 17:2-4).

All things preached in the New Covenant message have their root in Abrahamic covenant.

Not only was the Gospel of Christ's redemption, preached beforehand in Abraham, there were other fundamental truths proclaimed as well.

- **Gospel** (Good News) was initiated and established in the Abrahamic Covenant. (Galatians 3:16-17)

- **Tithing** was initiated and established in the Kingdom rule of the Abrahamic covenant. (Hebrews 7:2)

- **The unconditional covenant of Grace** is found in the words in Genesis "…through your seed shall all the families of the earth will be blessed." (Genesis 28:14)

- **The hygienic law of circumcision and blood covenant** was introduced and established in Abraham. "Every man among you shall be circumcised." (Gen 17:10)

Difference Between the Law of Moses and the Abrahamic Covenant

Moses' revelation of God was one of wrath and judgement, meted against those who could not perfectly "keep the law." Moses and the law was a schoolmaster, showing man his inability to keep the law, live holy before God, and finally to introduce him to Christ. (Galatians 3:24)

Circumcision was given by Abraham as one aspect of the ultimate plan for the Kingdom which originated in Abraham. The Abrahamic covenant relates to the ultimate spreading of the Gospel of the Kingdom of God throughout the entire world i.e. "through your seed shall all the nations be blessed."

Kingdom Principle of Multiplying and Possessing

"Is not the whole land before you? Please separate from me; if you go to the left, then I will go to the right; or if you go to the right, then I will go to the left." (Genesis 13:9)

"For all the land which thou see, to thee will I give it, and to thy seed forever. And I will make thy seed as the dust of the earth: so that if a man can number the dust of the earth, then shall thy seed also be numbered. Arise, walk through the land in the length of it and in the breadth of it; for I will give it unto thee." (Genesis 13:15-17)

Abram's surrendering "his personal right of choice" sets forth a principle that speaks volumes about the Kingdom of God. It is

God that exalts, not man. Self-exaltation always comes to an end. When God exalts it is far reaching, going far beyond "the man" himself to a point of "divine increase." Abraham told Lot you choose first, and I will take what is left. It was after Lot made his choice and Abraham had surrendered his right of choice that God told Abraham to look towards the north, south, east, and west ...for all the land that your eyes can see is yours and your seed (offspring) will be enumerable as the dust of the earth."

"And I will establish my covenant between me and thee and thy seed after thee in their generations for an everlasting covenant, to be a God unto thee, and to thy seed after thee. And I will give unto thee and to thy seed after thee, the land wherein thou art a stranger, all the land of Canaan, for an everlasting possession; and I will be their God." (Genesis 17:7-18)

The physical land that the God gave to Abraham was the material aspect of God's promise, the least important part of the promise. Though it played a meaningful role to Abraham, and his direct descendants. Yet it is in the broader aspect of the Abrahamic covenant that relates to the Gospel of the Kingdom of God, which was the promise that God gave to make Abram the father of many nations. Also, God stated that through his seed (as we have already quoted in Galatians 3) that Christ is that seed by which all families shall be blessed. What a rich blessing, to be able to do as Abraham did that day when he gave Lot the first choice. The surrender of the personal right of ownership to take what is left is a divine principle of increase that is revealed in both the Old and New covenants.

SPIRITUAL PARALLEL OF THE NATURAL AND THE SPIRITUAL

There were natural descendants of Abram that were to be given the natural (physical) land. However, there are spiritual descendants (all who are of faith) that are to receive the spiritual promises. It is this broader promise of all nations being blessed

that God reveals the spiritual, redemptive, aspect of the Kingdom. In this is revealed the principle of surrender and multiplying; to go up in the Kingdom of God, one must go down in humility. To humble one's self and go down means that you will be exalted.

"After this I beheld, and, lo, a great multitude, which no man could number, of all nations, and kindred, and people, and tongues, stood

before the throne, and before the Lamb, clothed with white robes, and palms in their hands." (Revelation 7:9).

Here we see a great multitude of souls that have surrendered their rights of choice to God; that have been exalted.

"And every creature which is in heaven, and on the earth, and under the earth, and such as are in the sea, and all that are in them, heard I saying, Blessing, and honor, and glory, and power, be unto him that sits upon the throne, and unto the Lamb for ever and ever." (Revelation 5:13)

Many books have been written about the Abrahamic covenant, and it would be good for the student of the Word to do an in-depth study and search for truth, for only those who seek, knock, and search will be given a full understanding. Bible students should see that all things here pertain to the Gospel of Christ and the Kingdom of God and is related to the Abrahamic covenant, where all spiritual seed thought, such as promise, and everlasting covenant, originated.

"For if the inheritance be of the law, it is no more of promise: but God gave it to Abraham by promise." (Galatians 3:18).

A distinct picture of grace is revealed in the Abrahamic covenant and promise.

"For the promise, that he should be heir of the world, was not to Abraham or to his seed, through the law, but through the righteousness of faith." (Romans 4:13).

The promise here is further proof that grace was revealed in Abraham (Ephesians 2:12-13). The Abrahamic covenant does away with any idea of being saved by works of the law. So we see in the Abrahamic covenant the second manifestation of the Kingdom of God, which relates to the ultimate purpose of God.

THIRD MANIFESTATION - FIRST ADVENT OF CHRIST'S COMING

"For unto us a child is born, unto us a son is given: and the government shall be upon his shoulder: and his name shall be called Wonderful, Counselor, The mighty God, The everlasting Father, the Prince of Peace. Of the increase of his government and peace there shall be no end, upon the throne of David, and upon his kingdom, to order it, and to establish it with judgment and with justice from henceforth even forever. The zeal of the LORD of hosts will perform this." (Isaiah 9:6-7)

CHRIST - THE PERSON OF THE KINGDOM

In this we see the birthing of a divine governmental kingdom, and its everlasting increasing domain. Christ's coming ushered in the Kingdom. We have talked about the relationship between Adam and God as being a "picture" of what the Kingdom would be. God's relationship with Abraham provides us a photo of God's "purpose." Now we see Christ's coming as the third manifestation of the Kingdom of God that relates to the "person" of the Kingdom, the King who rules over all earthy Kingdoms.

Where there is kingdom there must be a personage – the King. The two manifestations of the Kingdom of God of which we have spoken has to do with the overall purpose of God's Kingdom on the earth. Christ's coming, His death, burial, and resurrection, introduced to the world the power of God that no demonic force can withstand. The powers of darkness will never recover from the blow delivered against it at Calvary.

"And they said unto him, In Bethlehem of Judaea: for thus it is written by the prophet. And thou Bethlehem, in the land of Juda, art not the least among the princes of Juda: for out of thee shall come a Governor that shall rule my people Israel." (Matthew 2:5-6; Micah 5:2)

The word governor[6] refers to a reigning king, the Person of the Kingdom.

Jesus was the King, is the King, and will be the King tomorrow, and throughout all eternity. Nothing could be said to prove this any more than the above scriptures. Though over the years, some have taught that Jesus came to the earth the first time as Savior, but not as King, that He will come again the second time as King and Judge. One would have to twist the scriptures to say that Jesus did not come as King Eternal at His first appearing. Jesus, the King came to planet earth and ushered in His Kingdom. The "Messiah King" credentials were three-fold; He came as Prophet, Priest, and King.

"The LORD thy God will raise up unto thee a Prophet from the midst of thee, of thy brethren, like unto me; unto him ye shall hearken." (Deuteronomy 18:15).

This is called the basic prophecy, which tells that the Messiah was to be the prophet. The spirit of prophecy foretold the event of the coming Messiah-Prophet. This prophet was to be the super prophet who would "reveal God to his people."

"Yea, and the prophets from Samuel and those that follow after, as many as have spoken, have likewise foretold of these days." (Acts 3:24)

"God, who at sundry times and in divers manners spoke in time past unto the fathers by the prophets, Hath in these last days spoken unto us by his Son, whom he hath appointed heir of all things, by whom also he made the worlds." (Hebrews 1:1-2)

In the Old Testament rituals and ceremonies, the truth of the coming Kingdom of God was **concealed**. But now, in the New Testament, is openly **revealed**. *"Christ being the express image of God's person." (Hebrews 1:3)*

---

[6] Governor: to lead; to command with official authority; prince rule. Strong's Exhaustive Concordance.

The word "express" according to the Greek is "kharakter", meaning a "graver," the tool or the character, engraving: character the figure stamped, an exact copy or representation. The writer is saying that in Christ we see the very nature and character of Yahweh God, thus the express image.

"Ye are the children of the prophets, and of the covenant which God made with our fathers, saying unto Abraham, and in thy seed shall all the kindred's of the earth be blessed. Unto you first God, having raised up his Son Jesus, sent him to bless you, in turning away every one of you from his iniquities." (Acts 3:25-26)

The writer of Hebrews is saying that God has spoken in the past, and has spoken to us through the Prophet, not just one of the prophets, but the Prophet. Christ stands alone in the order of prophets. The Bible student by all means should read and acquaint his/her self with the Book of John, for it is here that Jesus spoke many things of the Father. In John 10:30, Jesus said, "I and my Father are One," and again in John 10:38, "the Father is in me and I in Him." This is the Messiah Prophet revealing God to man. *"And without controversy great is the mystery of godliness: God was manifest in the flesh..." (I Timothy 3:16)*

"Phillip said unto him, Lord, show us the Father, and it is sufficient for us. Jesus said unto him, have I been such a long time with you, and yet have you not known me, Phillip? He that has seen me has seen the Father; and how do you say then, show us the Father? Do you not believe that I am in the Father, and the Father in Me? The words that I speak unto you are not of myself; but the Father that dwells in me, He does the works. Believe me that I am in the Father and the Father in me, or else believe me for the very works sake." (John 14:8-11).

To see Jesus is to see the Father, to know Jesus is to know the Father. For that purpose Jesus came to reveal every aspect of the Father's nature and character. He was the prophet of which the ancient prophets said would come. The finite mind of man cannot comprehend the magnitude of this truth, and one can speak, only sparingly on such a great truth, no other religion on earth can make such a boast as to, that their prophets prophesied hundreds of years before and were able to predict their prophet to be both Prophet and Savior.

"Jesus answered, neither has this man sinned, nor his parents; but that the works of God should be made manifest in him." (John 9:13).

Jesus healing the blind man manifested "the works of God." Again, we see Christ, the Prophet revealing God to the world.

"The woman said unto him, sir, I perceive that you are a prophet." (John 4:19).

Again we see the "the Prophet" revealing the secrets of the heart. This is another manifestation of the nature of God, which Jesus brought to light and manifested as a Kingdom grace.

THE MESSIAH - PRIEST REDEEMER

The second aspect of the Messiah's credentials is one of "Priesthood."

"And the Redeemer will come to Zion, and unto them that turn from transgression in Jacob, said the Lord" (Isaiah 59:20)

The prophet, Isaiah, uses the word "redeemer" which according to Strong's Exhaustive Concordance carries the meaning, "to be the next of kin, and as such to buy back a relative's property; marry his widow, to purchase, ransom, and redeem." Christ the Messiah had to bear the qualifications that met the requirements of the ancient prophets; which was the proof of His credentials. He was who He said He was. Over the centuries many have laid claim to being "the Christ" but without having the proper credentials. Jesus had them all. A redeemer priest is one who redeems, thus, revealing man's need to the Father.

"For we do not have a high priest who cannot sympathize with our weaknesses, but One who has been tempted in all things as we are, yet without sin." (Hebrews 4:15)

The word used here, "high priest" is in reference to the Old Testament Mosaic order which related to the High Priest of that day. He prefigured the coming Messiah who was to be the High

Priest that could be touched by the feelings of our infirmities. Strong's Concordance says that the word "touched" has the meaning "sympathy with, by implication, to communicate, have compassion, having a fellow feeling.

"So also Christ did not exalt himself to be made a high priest, but was appointed by him who said to him, "You are my Son, today I have begotten you, as he says also in another place, "You are a priest forever, after the order of Melchizedek. In the days of his flesh, Jesus offered up prayers and supplications, with loud cries and tears, to him who was able to save him from death, and he was heard because of his reverence." (Hebrews 5:5-7)

CHRIST AS INTERCESSOR

"But this man, because he continues forever, has an unchangeable priesthood. Therefore he is able also to save them to the uttermosts that come unto God by him, seeing he ever lives to make intercession for them." (Hebrews 7: 24-25)

Christ as Messiah Priest brings another aspect of His credentials into view in the Kingdom, an aspect of Priestly Intercession. The writer says in Hebrews, that Christ glorified not Himself. You will find this to be His very nature, in giving glory to the Father. No other religion, other than the Christian religion, can lay claim to such a thing – A Priest Redeemer, who makes everlasting intercession.

MESSIAH PRIEST ONCE FOR ALL

"And they truly were many priests, because they were not suffered to continue by reason of death: But this man, because he continues forever, has an unchangeable priesthood.

Therefore, he is able also to save them to the uttermost that comes unto God by him, seeing he ever lives to make intercession for them.

For such an high priest became us, who is holy, harmless, undefiled, separate from sinners, and made higher than the heavens; Who needed not daily, as those high priests, to offer up sacrifice, first for his own sins, and then for the people's: for this he did once, when he offered up himself." (Hebrews 7:23-27)

In this portion of scripture the writer sets forth Christ as Priest, an aspect of His intercession that is overwhelming, to say the least. It is called the principle of "uttermost salvation." The word "uttermost" means: fully ended, entire, completed, all manner of means, whatever, and whosoever. This simply means that there is no place that men can go in which the redemptive power of the High Priest cannot reach; there is no burden too heavy for Him to lift. It is impossible for man to not be redeemed when he comes to God through Christ. How wonderful to know that our King and Priest has an endless priesthood.

No other religion can lay claim to the fact that they have a priest who can intercede for, and redeem man, one who died a substitutionary death, taking man's place in judgement, and rising from the dead to execute his own will.

"But Christ being come a high priest of good things to come, by a greater and more perfect tabernacle, not made with hands, that is to say, not of this building." (Hebrews 9:11)

"Wherefore in all things it behooved him to be made like unto his brethren, that he might be a merciful and faithful high priest in things pertaining to God, to make reconciliation for the sins of the people." (Hebrews 2:17)

Here we have the principle of "rightful intercession." Not just anyone could become a high priest, not even in the Old Testament priesthood. This Priest Redeemer of which the prophet Isaiah spoke of in Isaiah 59 had to measure up to the standard that the Old Testament prophets prophesied, "Being "made like unto His brethren." This is the very strength of Christ's credentials.

The fact that he walked among men, feeling and experiencing the same joys and pain that His brethren felt and His existence as flesh and blood was one of the qualifying ingredients of His credentials. The truth of this has given inspiration to many ministers to preach the Gospel of the Kingdom of God, for truly our King is with man in his darkest hour. He is the "rightful intercessor," because He is man's brother.

WHAT IS THE GOSPEL OF THE KINGDOM OF GOD

"Now, brothers and sisters, I want to remind you of the gospel I preached to you, which you received and on which you have taken your stand. By this gospel you are saved, if you hold firmly to the word I preached to you. Otherwise, you have believed in vain. For what I received I passed on to you as of first importance: that Christ died for our sins according to the Scriptures, that he was buried, that he was raised on the third day according to the Scriptures, and that he appeared to Cephas, and then to the Twelve. After that, he appeared to more than five hundred of the brothers and sisters at the same time, most of whom are still living, though some have fallen asleep." (I Corinthians 15:1-6)

Paul the apostle states emphatically that the gospel speaks to the fact of "Christ's" dying for our sins, that he was buried, and he rose again on the third day according to the scriptures.

Our High Priest Redeemer was born of the virgin, Mary, died and was buried, and rose again, on the third day, and spoke of the things pertaining to the Kingdom of God (Acts 1:3) during his final forty days before His ascension, back to the father. This is the Gospel.

"And there are also many other things which Jesus did, the which, if they should be written every one, I suppose that even the world itself could not contain the books that should be written. Amen." (John 21:25)

The above scripture pretty well says it all. How could one possibly write all that which could be said (or should) be said about a King of such splendor and beauty. He came to this earth to manifest the Kingdom of His Father. What has been written about Him here is to say is only the beginning of what could be said. Yet, it is my prayer that we shall come to know more about Him. Jesus is the King. He is Savior and Redeemer, the "blessed and only potentate." (I Timothy 6:15).

FOURTH MANIFESTATION – THE CHURCH

"And Simon Peter answered and said, "Thou art the Christ, the Son of the living God." (Matthew 16:16)

These ten words are the most important words ever spoken by man. This was what Christ was longing to hear. After giving a general answer to the question, "of whom do men say that I am?" Peter's answer was based upon the revelation which the Father gave him, which was spoken of in ten words. The Lord responded, with the most profound words in the entire Bible; "And I say also unto thee, that thou art Peter, and upon this rock I will build my church; and the gates of hades shall not prevail against it. I will give unto thee, the keys of the Kingdom of

heaven and whatsoever shall bind on earth shall be bound in heaven; and whatsoever thou shalt loose on earth shall be loosed in heaven." (Matthew 16:18-19)

"I will build my Church..." – this is the culmination of all the Old Testament prophecies concerning the coming of the Messianic Kingdom of God. The Church is the ultimate creative ability of the Father. Christ has no higher aim or goal in mind than to "build the church", and herein is revealed His plan for the Kingdom of God. He could now say to the whole world, "I have a way in which I am able to manifest my Father's Kingdom on earth. I now have an official agent vested with full Kingdom authority – The Church."

Jesus, giving the keys of the Kingdom to the Church is the fourth manifestation of the Kingdom of God. A key is a tool that one uses to lock or unlock; any dictionary will bear this out. It makes sense that Jesus would not give the keys of the Kingdom without giving the Kingdom. Earlier I mentioned that the church differs from the Kingdom in the fact that the church is "the acting agent in charge of administrating the affairs of the Kingdom." The Church is invincible; she is also eternal. The Church speaks for the Kingdom, and can be located at particular locations, such as the local church.

The Kingdom of God is found in the accumulation of all local church bodies that are made up of born-again believers who are truly functioning according to God's plan.

"And He sent them to preach the Kingdom of God, and to heal the sick." (Luke 9:2)

"Jesus said unto them, let the dead bury their dead, but go thou and preach the Kingdom of God." (Luke 9:60)

"...and as you go, preach saying, the Kingdom of Heaven is at hand. Heal the sick, cleanse the lepers, raise dead, cast devils, freely you have received, freely give." (Matthew 10:7-8)

No apostle in the New Testament was commanded to preach the "church," instead; they were commanded to preach the Kingdom of God – Kingdom mentality as opposed to church mentality.

"The law and the prophets were until John: since that time the kingdom of God is preached, and every man presses into it." (Luke 16:16)

It is scripturally evident that the church is mandated to preach the Gospel of the Kingdom of God. She is mandated to reveal the Kingdom while demonstrating its power to heal the sick.

Chapter 8

Stages of Growth: Progression in the Kingdom

"And he said, so is the kingdom of God, as if a man should cast seed into the ground; And should sleep, and rise night and day, and the seed should spring and grow up, he knows not how. For the earth brings forth fruit of herself; first the blade, then the ear, after that the full corn in the ear." (Matthew 4:26-28)

In the above scripture, we see that there are indeed different stages of growth and maturity to the Kingdom. We see the blade, the head, and the full grain. Jesus is saying that when the seed (Word), is cast into the ground (human heart), the seed of the Kingdom of God is planted in the earth. And just as sure as the Kingdom is planted, it will mature and bring forth fruit. It matures in stages. Satan may try to stop the seed of the Kingdom from taking root – but is powerless to do so.

DIFFERENCE BETWEEN THE CHURCH AND THE KINGDOM OF GOD QUESTIONED

The Kingdom of God is "universal" the ecclesia "church" is a visible expression of God's Kingdom on the earth.

There are those who have been known to make quite a substantive difference between the Kingdom of God and the Kingdom of Heaven. I would warn all who study God's Word to refrain from arguing over such matters. God has called us to peace; therefore, we must become "dispensers of peace."

"The Kingdom of Heaven is liken unto a man which sowed good seed in his field; but while men slept the enemy came and sowed tares among the wheat, and went his way. But when the blade was

sprung up, and brought fort fruit, then appeared the tares also." (Matthew 13:24-26)

This parable again shows that the Kingdom of God was in existence in the earth, with the tares growing right alongside. Now, according to the parable, this condition lasts until "the time of the harvest." The Lord did not separate this scene into two seasons, a time for the tares, and a time for the wheat. Instead, He made it emphatically clear that the two would be allowed to grow alongside each other, so, here is a very clear picture that shows that the seed of the Kingdom of God (wheat) and the Kingdom of Darkness (tares) exists on earth at the same time.

"Another parable put He forth unto them saying, the Kingdom of Heaven is like to a grain of mustard seed, which a man took a sowed in his field" (Matthew 13:31)

The Mustard seed represents "the unsolicited growth" of the Kingdom. The mustard seed, "the least of all seeds" has an insignificant beginning but matures to the point of having birds nest in her branches. This is another picture of the progressiveness of the Kingdom of God.

"Another parable spoke He unto them, the Kingdom of Heaven is like unto leaven, which women took and hid three measure of meal, until the whole was leavened." (Matthew 13:33)

According to Strong's Concordance the word, "leaven" means to ferment, as if boiling, to be fervid, or earnest. Leaven represents the "active" ingredient of the Kingdom as the seed represents growth in the Kingdom. The Kingdom had an insignificant beginning, in the eyes of the world, but that which might have had a small beginning was planted in the earth at the birth of Christ, and has been growing and expanding throughout the entire world and will continue to expand in the earth until she has influenced every tribe of people on the earth.

Jesus wanted His disciples to take note of the term "the Kingdom of God" because of the frequency of His using the term. The terms,

Kingdom of God, Kingdom of Heaven, Kingdom of Christ, Kingdom of the Father, are synonymous.

THE KINGDOM OF DARKNESS IS POWERFUL...
THE KINGDOM OF GOD IS MORE POWERFUL...

"Who (Christ) has delivered us from the power of darkness and has translated us into the Kingdom of His dear Son." (Colossians 1:13)

The Kingdom of Darkness is powerful, influencing masses of souls causing them to live in the realm of darkness. But the Kingdom of God is more powerful. Paul does acknowledge the power of darkness, that it holds sway over multitudes of souls; while at the same time saying that we have been delivered from its power and translated into the Kingdom of His dear Son.

It has been said, and rightly so, that "although Satan has been defeated, he still has a voice," by which he makes loud boastings throughout the world offering an alternative kingdom of darkness, by which multitudes of innocent, and unstable souls have been deceived and brought into captivity.

MANDATE, MESSAGE, AND METHOD

"And He sent them to preach the Kingdom of God and to heal the sick." (Luke 9:2)

The Mandate: is formerly a charge to a nation from a league of nations, authoritative as a sovereign order, charge.

The Message: is the preaching of Christ, and all that he is, to all ethnic groups. One should remember that the Father does not confirm "with signs following" when the message we preach is watered down and not proclaimed in power.

The Method: by which we proclaim the Gospel of the Kingdom of God, is by power and demonstration of the Spirit. (I Corinthians 2:4-5)

Mandate

As stated before, the Lord commanded His disciples to preach the Gospel of the Kingdom, which is not an option but a command. The church has no choice but to preach the Gospel of the Kingdom. Christ's word to the Church is the final authority. She must announce to the entire world that the Kingdom of God is come.

"...and this gospel of the kingdom shall be preached in all the world for a witness unto all nations, and then the end shall come." (Matthew 24:14)

Again, the reference to preach means to announce, proclaim, and publish the good news of the Kingdom to the entire world.

Jesus commanded the twelve to announce that the Kingdom of Heaven is at hand, they were to manifest the Kingdom's presence by healing the sick, cleansing the lepers, raising the dead, and casting out devils. The healing and raising the dead is a visible witness of the Kingdom of God's presence.

Message

The message is Christ, there is no other name given under heaven whereby man can be saved." His death and blood atonement for the sins of the world is the message. Sermons on faith, prosperity, and heaven or hell are only interjections into the broader picture of the Lord Jesus. That is our message.

"For if he that cometh preaches another Jesus, whom we have not preached, or if ye receive another spirit, which ye have not received, or another gospel, which ye have not accepted, ye might well bear with him." (II Corinthians 11:4)

Jesus Christ the redeemer of mankind is the message. However, Paul spoke of another Jesus. Is there really another Jesus? The answer to this question is yes. It is recorded that there is another Jesus who appears to people in occults. People who deny the virgin birth, and the efficiency Christ's blood. A Jesus that has been known to manifest himself at times who supposedly brings them a message. And there are those who claim that he is the blood-brother of Lucifer, and that his birth was the result of God (Elohim) having had a physical relationship with the Virgin Mary. This being the case then we must conclude that Satan perpetrates a deceptive lie through a demonic manifestation of another Jesus.

I am aware that Paul's reference to, "another Jesus" also has to do with Jewish Christians that believed in Christ, but taught that the only way to be saved was to observe the Mosaic laws such as circumcision, keeping of the Sabbath, etc. They could not accept the simplicity of the Gospel of Christ, thus complicating the gospel by believing that the Lord Jesus is not the Jewish Messiah and believing with those who said that the only way one is saved is by being circumcised.

"For by grace are ye saved through faith; and that not of yourselves; it is the gift of God." (Ephesians 2:8)

The message of grace is the message that binds Satan and renders him helpless. How can he have any power or authority when it is apparent that the "works of man" has nothing to do with salvation. It is in this area that Satan has always caused mankind to "shipwreck" his salvation. He is forever accusing man of being "unworthy of God's salvation," therefore; it depends on which voice one is going to believe; God's Word – or Satan's lie.

The Church is mandated to preach the message of love – God's love. The King stands among us patiently, and confidently observing His growing, and expanding Kingdom.

"I charge thee therefore before God, and the Lord Jesus Christ, who shall judge the quick and the dead at his appearing and his kingdom; Preach the word; be instant in season, out of season; reprove, rebuke, exhort with all longsuffering and doctrine." (II Timothy 4:1-2)

Think through this book before you write off the significance of the message of the Kingdom of God. The epistles, or letters, that were written to the churches of that day and sent to the seven churches of Asia, have everything to do with the message of the Kingdom of God.

In the past few years, we have seen a number of those who seem to believe that one must be able to prepare great sermons on healing, faith, and prosperity. Though healing, faith, and prosperity are a part of the gospel, it would be the height of ignorance to believe that this is our central message. When preaching the Gospel of the Kingdom of God, signs and wonders following is "the message."

METHOD

So the mandate to preach the Gospel is an irrevocable command and not a suggestion. The message of Christ and nothing short of proclaiming Him to a dying world will suffice. This shows us how to present to the world a viable witness. This is what gives the Christian preacher the right to believe that people should believe the message of the Gospel of the Kingdom of God is the absolute truth over and above what other religions have to offer or believe.

"and my speech and my preaching was not with enticing words of man's wisdom, but in demonstration of the Spirit and of power; that your faith should not stand in the wisdom of men, but in the power of God" (I Corinthians 2:4-5)

"Ye men of Israel, hear these words; Jesus of Nazareth, a man approved of God among you by miracles and wonders and signs, which God did by him in the midst of you, as ye yourselves also know" (Acts 2:22)

"By stretching forth thine hand to heal; and that signs and wonders may be done by the name of thy holy child Jesus." (Acts 4:30)

The above scripture verse is part of a prayer which Peter the apostle and other disciples prayed after having been threatened and ordered not to speak in the Name of Jesus anymore.

"God also bearing them witness, both with signs and wonders, and with divers miracles, and gifts of the Holy Ghost, according to his own will?" (Hebrews 2:4)

The early Pentecostal church witnessed signs and wonders as they preached the Gospel of the Kingdom of God, while many of the historical churches were resisting the Holy Spirit, and stopped preaching the powerful Gospel of Kingdom. The results of this change, was and is, the deadness that is prevalent in many churches throughout the world today.

"Long time therefore abode they, speaking boldly in the Name of the Lord, which gave testimony unto the Word of His grace, and granted signs and wonders to be done by their hands" (Acts 14:3)

"And these signs shall follow them that believe; in My name shall they cast out devils; they shall speak with new tongues." (Mark 16:17)

SIGN SEEKERS

No one can deny that supernatural signs and wonders occurred as the early church proclaimed the Gospel of the Kingdom. The power and authority that was given to the church was demonstrated in just such manner. Preaching the Gospel of the Kingdom and demonstrating its power and authority is the way in which the Gospel is to be preached. We are not to be "sign seekers - that is, we are not to seek signs over, and above, seeking the Lord Himself. There should be an overwhelming desire in each Christian's heart to see God's people healed of their infirmities for the healing of the sick and the working of miracles is the evidence that the Kingdom of God is presently at hand.

WORLD EVANGELISM IN RELATION TO THE ABRAHAMIC COVENANT

One cannot see the fullness of the Kingdom of God preached throughout the world, in power, without relating to the

Abrahamic covenant. The promise and covenant which the Father made to Abraham. The Church being the extension of the Abrahamic covenant, i.e. "all families of the earth shall be blessed" i.e. "father of all nations."

In 65 years of fulltime preaching ministry, we witnessed the greatest anointing of the Holy Spirit and its power demonstrated, while preaching the message of the "present tense aspect of the Kingdom of God."

LEADERSHIP IN THE KINGDOM

"For I think that God has displayed us, the apostles, last, as men condemn to death for we have been made a spectacle to the world, both to angels, and to men." (I Corinthians 4:9)

The apostle might have had in mind, that the one, whom God ordained to administrate the affairs of the Kingdom, could be likened unto one that is chained to the oars of a slave ship. All on board, including the captain, would be allowed to abandon the sinking ship" but not those who are condemned to die while chained to the oars, they could only keep on rowing and go down with the ship. A true leader stays with the ship through the storm; she or he will never abandon ship.

"And the children of Israel wept for Moses in the plains of Moab thirty days: so the days of weeping and mourning for Moses were ended. And Joshua the son of Nun was full of the spirit of wisdom; for Moses had laid his hands upon him: and the children of Israel hearkened unto him, and did as the LORD commanded Moses." (Deuteronomy 34:8)

No one can rule that has not been ruled, no one can lead that has not been led. Joshua submitted his life to God under Moses, his spiritual father and mentor. It was only because of a

servanthood attitude that Joshua was qualified to lead the Israelites to cross Jordan and into the Promised Land. Moses imparted the vision of entering the promise land to Joshua, the next generation, by laying his hands upon Joshua and so transferring the authority to lead.

One could not find a more perfect example of one generation of leaders passing full authority to administer the affairs of the Kingdom of God than is recorded in Deuteronomy, Chapter 34. The need for spiritual fathers who know how to pass on to the next generation spiritual authority to lead God's people into the next generation is vital if we expect to see a rebirthing of "the true apostolic ministry" in our day.

The Wisdom of Wise Sayings

- No one can rule that has not been ruled.

- No one can lead that has not been led.

- No one has been given authority that has not submitted to authority.

- Let no great men put too much trust in their greatness. The longer their robe, the more soil it contacts.

- Great power may prove to be the mother of great damnation.

- Success is measured, not so much by the position one has reached in life as by obstacles, which he has overcome while trying to succeed.

- Let all men that are "called" to administer the affairs of the Kingdom of God be done only by those who "tremble at His Word," while ascribing all greatness "to

- the Lamb that was slain from the foundation of the world."

GOOD TIMBER BY WOOD AND STREAM

by Douglas Malloch

The tree that never had to fight
For son, sky and air and light,
That stood out in the open plain,
And always got its share of rain,
Never became a forest king
But lived and died a scrubby thing.
The man who never had to toil
Heaven from the common soil,
Who never had to win his share,
Of sun and sky and light and air,
Never became a manly man,
But lived and died as he began.
Good timber does not grow in ease;
The stronger wind the tougher trees,
The farther sky the greater length,
The more the storm the more the strength;
By sun and cold, by rain and snows,
In tree or man good timber grows –
Where the thickest stands the forest growth
We find the monarchs of both
And they hold converse with the stars
Whose broken branches show the scars
Of many winds and much of strife –
This is the common law of life.

To whom is given the right and the authority to administer the affairs of the Kingdom of God, and to preach the Gospel of the Kingdom to all nations? The answer is given to us by Luke, *"In the last days, God says, I will pour out my Spirit on all people. Your sons and daughters will prophesy, your young men will see visions, your old men will dream dreams; Even on my servants, both men and women, I will pour out my Spirit in those days, and they will prophesy. I will show wonders in the heavens above and signs on the earth below, blood and fire and billows of smoke." (Acts 2:17-19)*

The question as to whom God will use to preach the Gospel of the Kingdom is:

- Age – young and old men
- The question of gender – menservants and maid-servants
- And they shall prophesy

When one truly accepts Christ, the Holy Spirit comes to dwell within, and assists that person. When the Holy Spirit is poured out upon the believer, it is for others. "The Great Commission" - to preach the Gospel of the Kingdom, heal the sick, cast out demons, and raise the dead, which is the standard of operation that is required to manifest the power of God's Kingdom.

The Church is commissioned by the Lord to minister on the same level of authority as Christ. In His authority, all things are possible. His Kingdom come, His Will be done, on earth even as it is in Heaven. Amen!

Conclusion

I conclude these few pages by saying that I have barely begun to proclaim just how important the message of the Kingdom of God is; I have introduced the alternate teaching as opposed to the end time teaching that is so prevalent to the Body of Christ today. Hopefully, you have been challenged to preach the Gospel of the Kingdom of God and renew Christ's command, that "this Gospel of the Kingdom shall be preached."

It is my desire that those who read this book will be able to recognize the present tense aspect of the Kingdom of God and to see Christ lifted up.

About the Author

Joseph Thornton, born June 14, 1929, resides in the United States.

Attended International Bible College, San Antonio, TX; married Katheryne after graduation and entered into full time ministry.

Joseph ministered in fifteen states in the U.S. and in eleven countries abroad helping to plant and establish a number of apostolic churches. At the age of 89, he continues to actively minister to a number of spiritual sons as an apostolic father.

www.ingramcontent.com/pod-product-compliance
Lightning Source LLC
Chambersburg PA
CBHW061501040426
42450CB00008B/1447